STANLEY GRAUSO

In Loving Memory of my Beloved & Beautiful Wife, The Late Rita Grauso.
May 03, 1916 – January 09, 1990

Special thanks to my son, Alexander Grauso II
and Gerald W. Isaac

On The Lam

INTRODUCTION

Saturday morning sunlight rests on a small neighborhood within the city of Bridgeport. Several houses sit at a distant within eye's view proximity of each other. A small well kept cape, except for its butchered but slightly manicured landscape, sits furthest out from the other homes in the area.

The screen door opens. An elderly man, known to some as Stanley Grauso, stands in the doorway. Lingtoy, Stanley's coffee shaded Siamese, exits onto a small porch area and makes his way over to a well prepared bowl of milk and cat food.

"There you go Ling," Stanley gestures, while looking down at his faithful companion. He smiles as the screen door closes, brushing against the top of Lingtoy's torso. At that moment, Lingtoy's purr toward his master sounds very much similar to the cooing of a newborn baby toward its mother.

Stanley makes his way over into the kitchen. He places his hand on the oak table by the wall for support, leans over a chair and takes a peek out of the window. Several underwear, a pair of trousers and a couple of sweaters hang on a makeshift clothesline

1

outside.

"Almost dry," he whispers to himself. Stanley pulls out his chair after pouring himself a glass of orange juice.

"Gotta' stay busy, gotta' stay busy..." he mutters upon taking his seat at the kitchen table. Mr. Grauso pridefully stares down at the breakfast prepared by him. Waffles, two eggs scrambled soft, sausage, orange juice and a small cup of coffee. Steam flies from the sausage as Stanley breaks into it with his fork. His hand twitches as he puts the food to his mouth but his motion remains steady. His frame, slightly overweighted but his posture, upright. Eggs spill off of the fork onto Mr. Grauso's pants which appear to be pulled slightly over his belly button while hugging his stomach. Stanley brushes the eggs onto the floor then vigorously scratches away at the spot trying to remove the small grease stain caused by the eggs.

It's nine thirty - five am by the clock centered over the window on the wall. Stanley has already showered, dressed himself, started a second load of laundry, cooked breakfast, fed his precious Siamese, Lingtoy, and taken a pack of chicken quarters out of the freezer to thaw. **NOT BAD FOR A NINETY - NINE YEAR OLD MAN**. Wouldn't you say?

Though up in age, Stanley Grauso, in spirit, exemplifies anything but that of an over the hill old man. Stanley turns his cup of coffee up for a final sip. The phone rings. The ring volume is set on blast.

"Who the hell is this?" He says making his way to the phone. Stanley adjusts his hearing aids and with the grip of a forty year old, he snatches the phone.

"Hello.....I said Hello...Who is this?" An automated voice on the other end comes into play. "Please hold...we have an important call for you. Don't hang up. Someone will be with you..." Without hesitation, Stanley slams the phone down.

"Those damn telemarketers..." Stanley walks away from the phone then suddenly remembers.

"Almost forgot", he says snapping his finger. Stanley then makes his way over to the kitchen cabinet furthest to the right. Upon opening it, he pulls out a Trader Joe's Blueberry Preserves jar containing water in it and a small pamphlet. Written on the pamphlet in gold writing is...WITHIN THE SANCTUARY...THE MASS. Stanley places the items onto his kitchen counter. He opens both the preserves jar and the pamphlet. Stanley then begins his usual morning religious ritual. He takes a few drops of water and sprinkles it onto himself head first then each shoulder in the notion or form of a crucifix.

"In the name of the Father... and of the Son... and of the Holy Spirit." The pamphlet is opened to page five, THE ORDER OF MASS. It appears to be book marked by a few smaller items. One of the items is a small two and a half inch by one and a half inch laminated card containing the image of St. Anthony. Stanley places the card of St. Anthony on the counter to his right. He recites, "St. Anthony, please bless my wife."

Stanley then pulls from the pamphlet a small obituary article cut from a newspaper. The article appears to have some wear and tear but it is obvious that it is precious to him. He kisses it, and places it down on the left side of the counter while smoothing out its crinkled and folded edges. In Loving Memory of My Wife, **RITA GRAUSO**, May 3, 1916 - January 9, 1990. Wife, Mother, Friend. He stares at the small black and white image of Rita. Her hair done up in a Bee Hive style; mixed with beauty and gracefully aging features. This woman was clearly a class act on her own.

"You were good to me...Rita...You definitely were good to me." He closes the blueberry jar of holy water. He gathers the picture of St. Anthony along with Rita's obituary and places them both back into his order of mass pamphlet. He then returns the items back into the kitchen cabinet.

The morning has anything but concluded for Mr. Grauso. His son, Alexander Grauso II, named after Stanley's father , has long left for the day to run his personal training business located in a nearby suburban town. There is not a home-maker, meals on wheels delivering to the elderly, or a visiting nurse in site. And there won't be one if Stanley Grauso continues to have any say so about it. Even though Stanley is alone, there is nothing about his mettle that breeds loneliness. No Sir! Two things you'll never hear Stanley Grauso argue about and that's religion or being left to himself. In fact, Stanley makes it his business to tell anyone fortunate enough to cross his path - in his deep Italian accent, "All my life I lived on the lam...and when ya' live on the lam...you gotta' live alone...He beats his chest and in conclusion says, "And that's why ...I GOT NO PROBLEM BEING ALONE..."

As Stanley makes his way into the living room his interests and pastimes become quite obvious. This guy is a DIE HARD YANKEES FAN. Pictures taken with several players such as Mike Mussina, Jason Giambi and Hideki Matsui as well as other monumental pieces of Yankee paraphernalia all grace Stanley's living room. One picture in particular taken at the stadium on Stanley's ninetieth birthday shows the Yankee score board in lights...HAPPY BIRTHDAY STANLEY GRAUSO. Puts a smile on Stanley's face to this very day.

Other interests that appears quite obvious is his love for the Italian style mafioso films. A huge canvased painting of Marlon Brando, The Godfather is stationed on an old eighties style couch off to the left. Pictures of The Goodfellas, The Sopranos and Scarface all take up space that isn't occupied by The New York Yankees. Hanging on the wall next to the painting is a collectors item , a picture plaque of Dale Earnhardt in the car moments before his fatal crash in Turn 4 on the final lap of the 2001 Daytona 500. The picture was given to Stanley by Dale's son, Dale Jr. Stanley takes a seat in his favorite chair. He pops a tape into the VCR and presses play. An image of Stanley comes on the screen dancing in the stadium aisle at Yankee Stadium. His moves really aren't that bad for a ninety-year old. Stanley just laughs while getting a kick out of himself.

Things haven't always been this pleasant for the elderly bundle of joy resembling an older version of Robert De Niro slash Danny DeVito. Although somewhat subdued and calm, his life has been anything but what it is now. Stanley glares over at an early photo of he and Rita. Funny, but the two in their earlier days show a striking resemblance of the charismatic George Raft and the lovely beautiful Vivien Leigh. Even their photos seem to gleam with that old black and white on camera romance type of feel. Had it not been for Rita, who knows where Stanley would be today. Every picture, every monumental piece inside this little sanctuary created by Stanley speaks its own volume concerning the well rested yet vigorous old man. Others may view certain artifacts as mere poster-boy images for the old organized crime scene but for Stanley, some things are a clear reminder of what life use to be. Old neighborhoods, nightlife, underworlds, running buddies, good times, bad times and a few regrets as well. In the sum of it all, clearly, they are reminders of life as it was for Stanley Grauso; *On The Lam.*

CHAPTER ONE

Alexander Grauso stood in the waiting area of St. Vincent's Medical Hospital, hat in hand and a ball of nerves. Taking deep breaths, he thought to himself, "Maybe this one's a little girl." He pondered for a moment, thinking of several names for his expected little angel. His hat looked like an old dish rag from hours of constant squeezing and ringing while Mrs. Grauso was in labor.

It was July 1st, 1912. In those days, fathers rarely went into the delivery room to watch the birth of their children. You can imagine the joy on Alexander's face when the mid-wife came out to inform him, "It's a boy Mr. Grauso!" Alexander just stood there wearing a smile from ear to ear.

"Aren't you going to say something? Don't just stand there!" The mid-wife exclaimed. Mr. Grauso then retorted with a smile, "Take me to my boy." As Alexander walked into the room, the door slowly closed behind him. Nestled in Josephine's arms was their new fourteen pound, three ounce bundle of joy. Alexander anxiously approached his wife and kissed her on the cheek.

"Another boy, huh babes? Will ya' look at this one!"

"And a stubborn one at that...this one didn't want to come out." Josephine appeared exhausted, dozing off a bit between words. Alexander reached over and took hold of his newborn son. He cradled, then kissed him numerous times.

"So how do you think Salvatore is gonna' take to his little brother?" (Salvatore is Alexander and Josephine's firstborn.) "They'll both be fighting for first place with you, that's for sure.", Josephine said.

"No need." Alexander replied with a smile. "I got enough space in this heart for ten children." Josephine raised both eyebrows.

"Are you trying to tell me something Alex?"

"Who knows?" Alexander jokingly replied. The couple laughed. Alexander Grauso then held his son to his ears pretending to hear words muttered by the newborn.

"He says that his name should be Stanley."

"And how does he know what his name should be?"

"Because like his father, he's going to be his own man." Alexander said.

"Then Stanley it is." Said Josephine.

At that moment, a well dressed young man in his early twenties entered the room. Josephine looked up toward her husband. Her expression signified that she had never seen the man before. Upon entering, the young man remained close to the door. Alexander placed young Stanley back into the arms of his mother and approached the young man. The two talked in a low muttering, whispered tone . Periodically, the young man referred to Alexander as *"Charlie"*. Alexander looked over his shoulder toward Josephine every now and then. Josephine couldn't quite make out what the men were talking about. Neither did she try. In those days wives pretty much made it their business to stay out of their husband's affairs. She could, however, make out the final words of her husband as his body language became a bit more stern toward the young man.

"I don't give a shit how important you think it is. Don't you ever fucking come around me when I'm wit' my family. You got that?" The young man nodded fearfully.

"Sorry boss." The young man left the hospital room in a hurry. Alexander turned toward his wife, smiled, then continued on as if nothing had ever happened. He and Josephine went on enjoying their new baby. Josephine dared not mention the issue of the young man to her husband.

★★★★★★★★★★★★★★★

By the time Stanley was ready to attend school, he was quite the child and had already developed a unique but fitting personality of his own. Josephine and Alexander often butted heads concerning Stanley. She often accused Alexander of favoring Stanley over Salvatore as if he were the oldest. Josephine often stated that her husband was "wrapped around Stanley's little finger," because Stanley, even at four years old, did whatever he wanted to do. Alexander, many times, would just shrug it off by saying, "Nonsense, I

3

wear the pants in this house."

In September of 1916, Stanley's mother enrolled him in Wheeler Elementary School, located on 40 Highland Avenue in Bridgeport, Connecticut. Stanley often complained about school saying , "I'd rather stay home with Papa." Some days Alexander would give the young lad his wish. By the time Stanley was four, Alexander was a very well respected man in the community. Even the truant officers, many times looked the other way upon seeing young Stanley in the streets during school hours. By the time Stanley was seven, he could easily sense the deep reverence others within the community had for his father and on several occasions used it to his advantage.

One Saturday morning, Stanley and his older brother, Salvatore, were on their way to the corner grocery store up the street from where the Grauso's lived. The store's owner was an elderly man, approximately eighty years old, by the name of Mr. Isaac Goldberg . Mr. Goldberg's eyes were failing him pretty badly but he often worked the store along with his daughter Carol to keep busy. Carol also served the purpose of looking after her elderly father during day to day store operations. Stanley and Salvatore approached the store's entrance. Before entering, Salvatore turned to his little brother and pleaded with him.

"We don't have any money and Mama says not to go into places like this if we don't have any money." Stanley quickly opened his hands revealing his small fortune to his brother.

"Don't worry about it. I've got plenty of money," said Stanley. Salvatore's eyes almost popped out of his head.

"Is that two dimes? Where did you get that Stanley? You better had not stolen that from Papa." In those days, twenty cents was a bit too much for any seven or eight year old to have.

"Nonsense." Stanley replied sporting a devilish grin. Stanley's right hand opened slowly. What appeared to be twenty cents was only two pennies craftily covered in foil.

"I don't like this Stanley," said Salvatore. "We can go to jail.".

Stanley shook his head.

"Stop being a pussy. I've done this before. Here's what we do. We be extremely nice

to the lady so she don't think nothing...ya' see? Then we wait until the old man is by the register ...cause he don't see so well... give him the fake money, get our change back and scat. You got that?" Stanley then shoved one of the makeshift dimes into a reluctant Salvatore's hand. "Now follow me and don't screw up!"

Both boys went into the store. Stanley made his way into the aisle where the cookies and candy were. Two huge cookies were only a penny. Stanley placed them in a plastic bag.

"Get yourself something too," he instructed Salvatore. Salvatore, however, refused. Stanley also picked up a couple of packs of Swedish fish candies. They too were two for a penny. He tried handing them to Salvatore in hopes that Salvatore would go along with his plan.

"You're crazy, and when you go to jail, I'm going to tell Mama." Salvatore then shoved the foil wrapped penny back into Stanley's hand and proceeded to walk out door.

Mr. Goldberg's daughter watched from a distance as the two boys argued but never really gave any significant attention to the matter. Mr. Goldberg loved dealing with the children and since most of their purchases weren't of significantly large amounts, there was no need for Carol to oversee any cash exchanges. Stanley paid for the items, received eight cents change back in return and left the premises.

Stanley caught up with Salvatore before he could make it home.

"You better not tell Mama." Salvatore remained quiet. "What about our oath? You know, *frada mea*." Stanley asked. (*Frada mea* means my brother in Italian). Stanley then pulled a large cookie and a pack of Swedish fish candies from the bag and offered them to Salvatore.

"Here's your share." Stanley said with a smile. Salvatore stood looking intensely at his younger brother. After a while both boys burst into laughter. Salvatore took the items, biting immediately into the huge chocolate chip cookie. Stanley just shook his head nodding and laughing.

"Everybody's on the take."

"On the take? What's that?" Salvatore asked with cookie crumbs falling from his mouth like an avalanche. Stanley put his arms around his brother's shoulder.

"It's what Papa says all the time. It means everyone has their own price to keep quiet." Both boys laughed. Although willing to split the take, Salvatore still seemed a bit bothered by the whole thing. When the two brothers made it home, Stanley instructed Salvatore to finish eating the goods in a secret place out back in order to avoid being seen by Mrs. Grauso with anything from Mr. Goldberg's store.

CHAPTER TWO

Stanley's fourth and fifth grade years for Mrs. Grauso had become quite exhausting since she was the caretaker and disciplinarian of her home. Mr. Grauso rarely intervened in disciplinary matters concerning the children. Everything in that department always fell on Mrs. Grauso's shoulders. Salvatore was a model student but for Stanley, suspension notices and letters of concern, from Stanley's teachers, often made their way to the Grauso's home. Stanley had already mastered the art of forging his mother's signature, or intercepting the letters at the mailbox before Mrs. Grauso or Mr. Grauso could have the chance of reading them.

One evening before going to bed Stanley and Salvatore both sat up in their room; each on his own bed. Salvatore whispered to Stanley, "Guess what I have?"

"Who cares?" Stanley replied. Salvatore slid his hand under his pillow and slowly pulled out a sealed envelope. He waved it around in a tauntingly.

"It's a letter from Mrs. O'Neal for Papa." The announcement of a letter home from school did absolutely nothing for Stanley.

"So what! You give it to Papa, he'll only tell you to give it to Mama. Who cares!"

"Oh yeah, and Mama will ring your ears and get the wooden spoon and you know what that means." Stanley remained silent and unshaken by his brothers threats of what their mother would do. Salvatore blew into the top corner of the envelope in hopes of intimidating Stanley.

"Lets see what it says, shall we?" Salvatore opened the letter trying his best not to destroy the sealed portion of the envelope. He opened it and began to read, "Dear Mr. Grauso, It - has - been...." Salvatore struggled with Mrs. O'Neal's cursive handwriting. Stanley just laughed.

"You can't even read and now if you show Mama or Papa, you'll get in trouble for opening it." Salvatore continued to stare at the letter.

"I know it says something about some kid ratting you out about taking money. This ain't good Stanley and when Papa hears about you taking money from other kids, you're bound to get it for sure." Immediately, Stanley sprung up from his bed.

"Give it to me!" Salvatore stood on his bed holding the letter over Stanley's head. Stanley persisted, "I said give it to me...or I'll..." Stanley balled up his right fist. Salvatore stepped down from the bed and leaned in pressing his face against his little brother's face.

"Or else you'll what..." Stanley remained quiet as he slowly unclenched his fist.

"That's what I thought... Nothing." Said Salvatore. While there were a lot of kids in the neighborhood who feared Stanley, his brother Salvatore wasn't one of them. Both boys stood in their undershorts. Stanley then began pleading with his brother for the letter. Salvatore continued to give Stanley a hard time about the letter.

"Why do you as Mama says...make her hairs grey? Why do you get into so much trouble Stanley?"

"I like trouble..." Salvatore stared at his brother in amazement.

"What do you mean...you like trouble? How can anyone like trouble?" Stanley fanned his hand in a sarcastic manner toward Salvatore.

"There you go with your goody two shoe answers." He said. "I like trouble and I want to be a hood...Now give me the letter."

"Are you crazy...be a hood? Papa will kill you." Stanley chuckled yet still remained serious about his answer.

"Well that's my answer and I'm sticking to it till the day I die. Now give me that damn note!" Stanley rushed over to his brother reaching for the letter sent by Mrs. O'Neal. Salvatore blocked Stanley with his forearm. The look on Stanley's face clearly stated that he wasn't going to be deterred from his answer.

"Stanley, think about what your saying..." Salvatore pleaded.

"What's there to think about?"

"Don't you get it? Papa will kill you!" Stanley shrugged it off slightly and walked away.

"Nonsense." He said.

"What do you mean nonsense? Papa wants no hoods for kids. He wants us to be like him: hardworking, honorable, respectful..." Stanley interrupted Salvatore's list of accolades.

"Mama wants those things. Not Papa."

Salvatore clenched his teeth, "Stanley Grauso you take that back." Stanley remained quiet.

"I said take that back." Salvatore retorted. Stanley then turned toward his older brother with a devilish grin that stretched a mile long.

"Papa's a hood...and a good one." Salvatore's eyes widened immediately striking Stanley across the face. Stanley responded with a quick punch to Salvatore's stomach. The boys began to tussle, ending up on the floor.

"You take back what you said." Salvatore shouted.

"I ain't taking shit back." Stanley replied with his head caught in a headlock. Mr. Grauso and a very pregnant Mrs. Grauso both burst into the room breaking the boys up. Mr. Grauso grabbed Stanley while Mrs. Grauso cuddled Salvatore. Salvatore poured it on a bit thick, holding his stomach. Mrs. Grauso continued rubbing his head while calming him.

"Honey, are you alright?"

"Yes Mama." Salvatore replied. Stanley watched with intensity as Mrs. Grauso continued to show affection towards Salvatore.

"I'M ALRIGHT TOO... YOU KNOW!" He shouted toward his mother. Mr. Grauso snatched Stanley by the arm.

"YOU WATCH YOUR TONE WITH YOUR MOTHER, YOUNG MAN!" Stanley seemed to calm down immediately. His expression, however, still remained cold and oddly tempered.

Stanley shrugged away as his mother reached to caress his face. Mr. Grauso looked at Mrs. Grauso and nodded. Mrs. Grauso received her cue and exited the room.

"Good night," she said quietly.

Both boys were alone with their father. Mr. Grauso smiled as he took his seat onto Stanley's bed. Neither Stanley or Salvatore knew what to make of their father's smile. Mr. Grauso, depending on the mood he was in, was a very hard man to read.

"So tell me, what's all this about?" At that moment, Salvatore noticed the note from Mrs. O'Neal balled up on the floor next to his foot. Stanley's eyes carefully shifted watching Salvatore drag the note with his foot under the bed.

"How bout' you Stanley? Do you want to tell me?" Salvatore blurted out, "It's nothing Papa. Just boy stuff... Right Stanley?" Stanley nodded questionably. Mr. Grauso chuckled a bit. He then insisted that the boys shake hands. Salvatore extended his hand first and the two shook hands. Mr. Grauso kissed his two sons on the head and watched as both boys crawled into bed. Salvatore reached over his night stand and turned out the light. Throughout the night Salvatore often called out to Stanley whispering, "Stanley you awake?" Stanley, however, didn't respond even though he was awake. Stanley just laid on his back, hands behind his head staring upward toward the ceiling until he eventually fell asleep.

* * * * * * * * * * * * * * *

The next morning both boys walked to school. Salvatore on several occasions attempted to rekindle the subject of the conversation from the night before.

"You gonna tell me why you called Papa a hood or not Stanley?" Stanley sarcastically replied, "Hood? When did I call Papa a hood?"

"You're being funny Stanley. Now stop it!" Stanley placed both his fingers in his ears.

"La - La - La - La!" He sang loudly as Salvatore continued. The boys approached the school yard. Several children played games of kick ball and stick ball outside before the morning bell. Salvatore and Stanley both stood by a white gate with a loose picket board. Several children often used it as a short cut by shifting the board and cutting through the gate. Salvatore grabbed Stanley by the arm as he cut through the gate.

"Look Stanley, I won't let you go into school until you tell me why you would say such a thing about Papa." Stanley sighed deeply in aggravation as he pulled away from Salvatore.

"I MADE IT UP...NOW LEAVE ME ALONE ALREADY!" Salvatore stood speechless as the school bell rang. Stanley angrily walked away. Salvatore called out to his younger brother but Stanley kept walking and with his back turned shouted, "I SAID...I MADE IT UP! JUST DROP IT!"

Upon entering school, Stanley made his way into his classroom where Mrs. O'Neal greeted him.

"Good morning Stanley." Stanley didn't want to speak to Mrs. O'Neal, still angered by the note sent home by her. Stanley was a sucker for Mrs. O'Neal's resonating beauty and blue eyes. Stanley was adamant about being a tough guy so he kept his eyes on the floor in order to avoid eye contact with Mrs. O'Neal. Mrs. O'Neal just smiled as the little tough guy walked by without speaking. Stanley approached his desk and took his seat.

The weather was cold but fair enough for the kids to go out and play. The recess bell rang and Mrs. O'Neal instructed the children to line up. As each child passed, Stanley approached Mrs. O'Neal's desk. She stopped him.

"Stanley I need to speak with you." Stanley remained behind as the other children passed out into the school yard.

"Look at me Stanley." She said in a soft, motherly tone. Stanley took his eyes off of the floor.

"You know...it's good etiquette to look someone square in their eyes when speaking

14

to them Stanley." Stanley wrapped his eyes around Mrs. O'Neal's and melted. He didn't know whether to smile or stop breathing. One thing's for sure, this little boy was hooked. Mrs. O'Neal stepped from behind her desk. She placed her hand on Stanley's soft, chubby face and looked him square in the eyes.

"That's a boy," she said. "You see Stanley, when you look someone square in the eyes...that's how they know you mean business...You do want to be a good business man...don't you Stanley?"

"Yes ma'am," Stanley replied.

"Look Stanley." Mrs. O'Neal said. "If there's any more shenanigans with you and Joey Donatelli or anyone for that matter...It'll be a trip to Principal Peck's office. Do I make myself clear?" Stanley nodded in agreement without saying a word.

"Now run along..." Stanley smiled and started for the door. Mrs. O'Neal called out to Stanley, "And for goodness sake... have some fun for a change...will you?"

"I will." Stanley replied while running out into the school yard.

CHAPTER THREE

"Go away Stanley," several girls shouted. Stanley had approached the girls

tangling up their jump rope as they turned. Lisa Caruso shouted, "Stanley I'm telling Ms.

O'Neal." Stanley then picked up the hop scotch marker and threw it at Lisa. He laughed

and began making his way over toward his next victims, Joey Donatelli and George

Mallozzi. Both boys were standing by the broken fence. Joey Donatelli was known in

those days as a pretty boy. All the little girls adored him, sometimes to the point where it

made things complicated with the other boys in the school. George Mallozzi was known

simply as "Big George". Although big for his age, he was as soft as a cream puff. In fact,

that's what Stanley called him. Both boys seemed nervous upon Stanley's arrival.

"Alright pretty boy and cream puff...fork it over." Joey and Big George each went in

their pockets and pulled out a penny. Stanley snatched the money from each of them. He then turned to Joey and whispered, "I ought to bust you dead in the chops for that stunt you pulled getting me in trouble with Mrs. O'Neal." Joey leaned backward into the fence to avoid being hit by Stanley. "Don't worry, I ain't gonna' hit you..." Joey attempted to explain.

"Honest Stanley...I didn't mean to..." Stanley took one look over his shoulder then slapped Joey. Little Joey cried like a baby.

"Get a hold of yourself...And how many times I gotta tell you two bums to call me Charlie when we're doing business?" Joey just stood there holding his face red with embarrassment. Stanley had practically engraved a pink hand print on the side of Joey's face.

"Okay Charlie," both boys fearfully uttered. Big George stood trembling with the mannerism of a frightened little mouse. His eyes were practically begging Stanley not to do the same to him.

"Here's what we're going to do," said Stanley to Joey. "I want two pennies a week from you for that stunt you pulled." Both boys eyes lit up.

"C'mon Stanley...I mean Charlie..." said Joey. "I have a hard enough time stealing one penny from my mom's purse. How in the world am I going to come up with two? I think she's starting to notice..."

"That ain't my problem," Stanley shouted. "I guess you better start stealing the silver stuff. Got me?" Joey nodded in a very timid manner.

"It's either that or I stop taking up for the both of you. And you know what that means. Your little candy asses getting kicked everyday by the other punks in this joint." By now, Stanley had become a faithful practitioner of the eye contact rule learned from his teacher, Mrs. O'Neal. It had become his new weapon of intimidation. His fists, of coarse, were his second choice.

The recess bell rang and Stanley walked away. Joey and George remained a short distance behind in order to avoid Stanley.

"I swear, one day I'm going to kick his little chubby ass," Big George whispered. Joey Donatelli rolled his eyes upward and in a frustrated manner replied, "You can't even kick my ass George. How you gonna kick Stanley Grauso's ass?"

Later on that day Mrs. Grauso stood by the stove cooking dinner. Mr. Grauso sat off in his office with guests. Josephine Grauso was an amazing cook. To see her in the kitchen was like watching someone listen to his favorite song. A rhythm of passion and emotion stirred within her. It was the one place where she could drown out the occasional shouting often heard coming from her husband's office. It was her sanctuary, her alone time and an occasional escape from the cackling and fighting of children.

Salvatore occasionally sat around the kitchen helping his mother: cleaning up after her, picking fresh vegetables from the family's garden or sampling an occasional masterpiece in the making. Stanley, unlike Salvatore, loved being around Mr. Grauso, whenever he was home or deemed it appropriate for Stanley to be around him.

Alexander Grauso was a respected bondsman and worked in the court system as well. His influence among several elites within the community had definitely grown and so had his financial status. Mr. Grauso had purchased a three family house located at 153 Lexington Ave in Bridgeport, CT. Alexander had the home gutted and constructed to the fitting of his own liking and agenda. On the outside, the home pretty much kept with the typical style and fashion of a three family residential house. The front entrance to the house led directly to an open foyer and to Mr. Grauso's office. A small stairwell in the foyer led to other offices upstairs as well. Josephine and the kids were never allowed to use the front entrance but rather used the back entrance per Mr. Grauso's command.

Josephine's chicken tortellini with her famous butter and red sauce was ready. The scent permeated throughout the entire house. It even made its way into Alexander's office. Mr. Grauso prided himself on his wife's cooking. Josephine often cooked more than enough because her husband frequently had guests. It was only a matter of time before Alexander would storm into the kitchen, bragging in his deep Italian accent, "You gotta go to Italy for food like this!" To refuse Mr. Grauso's offer would be a complete insult, warranting one to be thrown completely out on his ass.

Dinner was finished. Mr. Grauso and his guests were completely stuffed. Alexander, along with his guests, excused themselves from the dinner table. His guests were two young couples from Italy. One of the young men spoke only in Italian.

"It was certainly a pleasure meeting you Mrs. Grauso... and your food...." The man kissed the tips of his fingers repeatedly saying, "Magnifico, magnifico!" Mrs. Grauso thanked the young man as everyone laughed and agreed. Alexander kissed his wife then moved his company back into his office. Salvatore helped his mother with the dinner dishes. Mrs. Grauso instructed Stanley to go upstairs and wash for school the next day. Stanley, however, made a detour. He hid himself between the door and the stairwell located in the foyer by his father's office. This had become a regular practice for Stanley. He listened as his father conducted business.

Mr. Grauso spoke to the young man who had complimented Mrs. Grauso's cooking. The young man, who spoke only in Italian at the dinner table spoke clear English behind closed doors with Mr. Grauso. The others literally knew no English at all.

In addition to being a bondsman, another one of Mr. Grauso's ways of making money was in helping immigrants attain legal status and find aide. Alexander's influence with Judge O'Malley afforded him a position in the court system as an interpreter. He was very instrumental in the Americanizing of several immigrants, in Connecticut and some parts abroad, during that time known as the Progressive Era. His efforts and favors to many called for loyalty in return; especially from his own family and his own kind.

"Now when we go to court tomorrow..." Mr. Grauso continued speaking in Italian. "No one is to know a stitch of English." The young man and the others nodded as he spoke.

"If anyone asks a question, just look at me. I will interpret. Do I make myself clear?"

20

Everyone agreed.

"Shit." Stanley whispered. He could hear someone coming through the front door. The sound of male adult laughter and conversation increased as the door swung open. He crouched down and shifted behind the stairwell in order to avoid being seen by the two men entering his father's office. One of the men appeared much older than the other and throughout much of the conversation said nothing. He just smiled and nodded most of the time. The younger of Mr. Grauso's guests did most of the talking. His name was Ernesto Cozza aka "*Don Ernesto Cozza*". Stanley remembered seeing Don Ernesto once or twice before. Alexander joked with the two men upon entering.

"Doesn't anyone fucking knock anymore?" Alexander's previous guests appeared a bit reluctant due to Don Ernesto's presence. He was no secret to many within the circles in which he and Alexander Grauso ran in those days. His operations in Bridgeport extended from cat houses, number rackets to bootlegging up and down the coasts of the United States and Canada. His friends and clients included some of the most affluent lawyers and politicians of his era. Considered a made man, city officials and public servants practically lived out of Don Ernesto's pockets. He always found a way of being too legal to touch and too feared to be crossed.

Both men took off their coats and continued conversing as Alexander walked the two couples to the front door.

"Can I interest the both of you in a drink?"

"Let me get to the point *Charlie...*" Don Ernesto referred to Alexander Grauso as *"Charlie"* in the presence of the old man. Stanley eagerly listened while crouched between the door and the stairwell. This wasn't the first time Stanley had heard anyone refer to his father, Alexander Grauso, as *"Charlie"*.

"I want you to stop this nickle and dime shit you're doing and join me in the rackets. You're too talented for small time honest work." Mr. Grauso remained calm.

"Thanks for the compliment Ernie, but we've talked about this. You know I don't do cat houses." Cat houses were upper class prostitution rings where prostitutes and their johns were housed. Mr. Grauso hated cat houses or anything to do with prostitution. In his words, "Pimps were low lifes."

"So leave the cat houses to me. The more the merrier." Don Ernesto asked that the old man wait outside.

"Look Alexander...if I can call you Alexander?" Mr. Grauso agreed to Don Ernesto's request.

"You are a very well respected man. I don't have to tell you that. You have the courts, all of the local politicians owe you favors, the community loves you..." Don Ernesto chuckled. "Hell...even the criminals love you...I love you. I trust you." Don Ernesto stood up and walked over to a window. "And I don't trust too many people Alexander...So what do you say?" Alexander Grauso thought to himself for a minute.

"If I decide to do this...it's gotta be on my terms...and my rules. I own me...No one

22

owns Alexander." Alexander placed his hand on Don Ernesto's shoulder.

"Can you deal with that Ernie?" Don Ernesto placed both hands on Alexander's face and spoke with the uttermost sincerity.

"Frada." Mr. Grauso nodded. The two men kissed each other on the cheeks, said their farewells and parted.

A very pregnant Mrs. Grauso stood hovering over Stanley. His attention was so drawn to his father and the two men that he didn't hear his her tipping in. Without hesitation she grabbed Stanley by his right ear and proceeded to ring it. Stanley screamed but Mrs. Grauso covered his mouth with the other hand and pulled him into the kitchen.

"How many times must I tell you, Stanley Grauso, your father's business does not concern you?" Stanley squirmed as if someone had stuck a match to his ear. Mrs. Grauso wasn't letting go.

"I'm - sorry - I - won't - do - it - again." He said pushing his words through his teeth. Mrs. Grauso reached into the kitchen drawer and pulled out a long wooden spoon. Stanley's eyes grew increasingly larger.

"I swear on everything I love," she said threatening Stanley with the spoon. "This will be your backside if I ever catch you in there again! Do I make myself clear, Stanley Grauso!"

"Yes Mama."

"Now go to your room and rest as I've told you."

23

At that time Mr. Grauso walked in. Stanley ran to him and greeted him with joy. Mr. Grauso's eyes always lit up whenever Stanley approached him.

"Hey little guy...Why aren't you in bed?"

"I wanted to stay up with you Papa." Mrs. Grauso interrupted speaking in a very stern manner to Stanley.

"I SAID GO TO YOUR ROOM!" Stanley stared at Mr. Grauso looking for him to override Mrs. Grauso's decision. Seeing that she was quite serious, Mr. Grauso looked at Stanley and in a joking manner replied, "I can't save you...your mother has spoken." Stanley then marched away in a small temper tantrum.

"What was that all about?" Alexander said to his wife. Josephine walked over and kissed her husband softly and slowly on the lips.

"It's nothing." Mrs. Grauso rested her hand on her husband's chest. "Go and take your shower. I'll be up on a minute, after I finish down hear."

"Sounds good to me," said Alexander as he trotted off whistling. Mrs. Grauso grabbed a dish towel and proceeded wiping down the kitchen table. Her rhythm of cleaning was interrupted for a moment as she stopped. Her thoughts were clearly focused on her once fourteen pounds and three ounce stubborn bundle of joy. Small breaths of energy seemed to leave her. Mrs. Grauso pulled out a chair. She sat silently to herself fighting the tears as they came. Finally, she caved in to her emotions and gave way to a mother's silent crying spell.

CHAPTER FOUR

S tanley's final years of school, surprisingly, had come in the sixth grade. His aggressiveness as a child had grown increasingly worse. His likes and dislikes for age appropriate child-like things seemed to have crossed paths with the inappropriate. Mrs. Grauso now carried the load and the responsibility of raising five children all together: Salvatore (eleven years old), Stanley (ten years old), Rose (eight years old), Dolly (six years old) and Freddy (five years old).

Mr. Grauso's status and involvement with Don Ernesto's underground activities in addition to running his own businesses and working took up most of his time. Some days he was home long enough to sleep and keep Mrs. Grauso pregnant. The school system adored Salvatore and his other sisters but with Stanley, they had practically given up altogether.

Principal Peck and the districts' superintendant thought it best as a last measure to place Stanley with a teacher by the name of Ms. Chichester. It was said by the districts' superintendant that Ms. Chichester had a way and a strong influence with kids like Stanley. Off record, the word was that she was as intimidating and tactical as a bulldog and that *by any means necessary* was the approach she took in rearing her kids in a classroom setting. Her two-hundred plus pound frame, unstylish hair and stagnated facial expressions seemed to be the proper motivator with headstrong inflexible children. Hearsay often speculated that Ms. Chichester had been physical with several children. There had been several behind closed door meetings with parents but the allegations never stuck because Ms. Chichester always remained employed by the school board with the districts' backing.

****

On October 31, 1919, the children in Ms. Chichester's classroom were having a Halloween party. Seeing more than ten children in Ms. Chichester's classroom smiling and actually having fun was rare. Even Ms. Chichester seemed to be in good spirits. Several children and even a few staff members often joked about Ms. Chichester being a witch. Halloween was the only day children were cut a little slack and colleagues were found in any good graces with the stern teacher.

Stanley asked that he be excused to the boys room. He was given a wooden board marked HALL PASS. The recess bell rang as Stanley made his way into the lavatory.

Upon flushing the urinal, he slipped in a small pool of piss left behind on the floor by other students. Stanley braced himself on the urinal to keep from falling. Unfortunately, his hand made it into the urinal part-way while the combination of water and urine made its way down the drain. Suddenly, a nervous voice blared out, "Hey, are you Charlie?"

"Who?" Stanley was completely caught off guard.

"Charlie...they said you're the man to come to when there's a problem...for protection?" Standing before Stanley was a young snot nosed, bifocal wearing, frightened little boy by the name of Reuben Ackerman. Reuben's frame looked like it would crack if you blew on him too hard. He looked like a hanger with a head the way his shirt fell off of his shoulders and swayed on his body. Even Stanley's stubborn heart moved with a miniscule amount of compassion toward Reuben.

"Oh...yeah... I'm Charlie...How the hell are ya?" Stanley extended the hand covered in piss and shook hands with the lad. Stanley then patted Reuben on the shoulder in an attempt to finish drying off his hand. The wet spot made by Stanley on Reuben's neatly pressed checkered button down twill instantly became an eyesore.

"Look kid...it's one cent to discuss the problem...two cents to take care of the problem. Got me?" Without batting an eye or saying a word, Reuben reached into his pocket.

"How's this ...it's a pretty big problem." Stanley's face lit up like a tree on Christmas day. Reuben flashed a crisp one dollar bill.

"Wow! Where did you get that?" Stanley asked (as if he really cared).

"My mom gave it to me to give to you. I told her about my problem and then I told her about you. She was totally cool with it."

"Step into my office." Stanley replied. Stanley ushered Reuben over to the stall furthest to the wall. Carved and scratched in the submarine blue chipped paint was the name Charlie White. Stanley Grauso had obviously marked his territory. The door hung oddly at an angle from its broken hinge. The two boys stepped into the stall.

"SHIT! Who the hell has been in my office?" Reuben pinched his nose like a vice grip while Stanley fanned the stench of a large day old turd floating in the commode. He and Reuben immediately exited Stanley's business quarters.

"Look... I can get you more if you can fix what's troubling me," Reuben said.

"You mean *who's* troubling you. Don't you?" Stanley replied.

"No, I mean *what's* troubling me."

"Sure!" Stanley reached for the small fortune in Reuben's hand. Reuben pulled back securing the dollar in a tightly closed fist.

"My Mom says, 'Not until you fix the problem.' Remember?"

"Okay...what is it that you want me to do?"

"Follow me." Stanley followed as Reuben led the way.

The boys approached Ms. Chichester's class. Stanley squatted down to avoid being seen and carefully crept by the main entrance to the office. The two headed out into the recess yard.

"Over here." Reuben shouted showing Stanley the way to Hell's gates. Reuben strutted in front of Stanley like a peacock. His lungs filled up with air and his demeanor dared anyone to mess with him. All he knew was that he had hired the enforcer, *Charlie White*.

"It's the new kid over here Charlie...they call him Bear." Stanley and Reuben approached a small crowd of kids crowded around the loose picket fence. One child in particular was crouched down on the ground shooting marbles. None of the children looked threatening or intimidating in any way to Stanley. A couple of the kids backed out of the way as Stanley stepped onto the scene.

"Which one of you bums got a problem with my little cousin Reuben here." No one spoke up at first. "I said who's the punk they call Bear...and someone had better start speaking up or I'm gonna start kicking everybody's ass over here." The kid crouched down playing marbles had his back turned toward Stanley. Cody Washington was his name. He spoke very softly.

"I'm Bear." Cody slowly turned around and stood up. His presence seemed to cast the shadow of nightfall over Stanley and Reuben. Stanley immediately thought to himself, "Reuben didn't tell me I had to fight a teacher." This kid seemed to grow right before Stanley's eyes. Bear was new to the neighborhood, an inter-racial kid only ten years old: too big, a little slow and too strong for his age. His clothes barely fit his one-hundred and ninety pound frame of solid slabs of fat and muscle mix. The other kids began backing away getting out of Bear's reach. Reuben trembled like a reef shaken by the wind.

"Any problem..." Reuben couldn't quite formulate his words due to his uncontrollable shaking. "Any - problem - with - me...you - take - it - up - with - my - cousin - Charlie - from - now - on - BEAR!" Reuben immediately shoved the dollar into Stanley's hand and in a flash sprinted off like a runner in a hundred mile dash. Stanley stood all alone in front of this mass of juvenile trouble. No one dared to help or even ran to go and tell a teacher and even if they could, they wouldn't have. Stanley had taken money and bullied so many of the kids at the school that a moment like today only looked like pay-backs from God for Stanley. Several of the kids even smiled while a few taunted Stanley singing with their teensy voices in a chorus fashion.

"Charlie's getting his ass kicked...Charlie's getting his ass kicked." Stanley quietly balled the dollar up and shoved it deep into his pocket.

"So you want to bring trouble my way...is that it?" Bear said to Stanley.

"Trouble?...I ain't got no trouble with..." Before Stanley could finish his sentence Cody Washington immediately showed Stanley Grauso why they called him Bear. Cody struck Stanley with his infamous bear claw. A couple of kids standing on the sideline wiped away the slob that flew from Stanley's mouth due to the impact of Bear's colossal blow. While Stanley remembered being hit, he didn't quite remember falling. One thing's for sure, his little ass was laid out on the ground face first.

"What the..." He thought to himself. Stanley scrambled trying to recover his equilibrium.

"No man is a match for....BEAR!" And boy was he right. Stanley Grauso was no match for Bear's strength. Cody Washington beat Stanley like a rag doll. After about the fifth slap and a series of body slams, Stanley landed right next to the loose picket in the fence.

"It's either kill or be killed..." He thought to himself. Stanley grabbed hold of the loosened picket and with a small wiggle and a tug was able to secure it for himself. He immediately jumped to his feet with Bear approaching still shouting his super-hero gibberish. Several of the kids watching backed away clearing more space to avoid Stanley's one-big giant swing for man kind. Stanley holding a huge slab of wood did nothing for Bear.

"So you have chosen your weapon...Bear needs no weapon!" Cody Washington lunged forward completely charging toward Stanley. Stanley moved to his right a little and took one swing. The picket landed perfectly on Cody Washington's leg behind the knee. He buckled instantly stopping like a car in a crash . Bear let out a scream that rang throughout the schoolyard into the school halls.

"OH MY GOD!" One of the kids shouted. "STANLEY'S GOING TO KILL HIM!" Cody kneeled on the ground holding the back of his leg.

"You ain't such a bear now...are you?" Revenge tasted better than his mother's cooking at this point. Stanley raised the old picket slab and struck Cody in the back with it. At that moment, several of the kids risked themselves by jumping into harms way.

"Get your candy asses out of the way or all of you can get it. Got me?" The kids wouldn't move. Cody stayed put on the ground holding his alleged injuries sustained by Stanley. Amongst the children taking up for Cody was little Lisa Caruso, who Stanley picked with frequently. Big George the cream puff and pretty boy Joey Donatelli. Big George and Joey shook in their boots. Little Lisa, however, sternly spoke up.

"If you hit him then you gotta' hit all of us." Stanley thought to himself for a second.

"Well...if that's how you want it toots." Stanley lifted the picket slab in a manner suggesting that he would take Lisa and the crowd of kids up on their offer.

"STANLEY GRAUSO!" A voice blared. Stanley hesitated.

"WHAT ON GOD'S GREEN EARTH DO YOU THINK YOU'RE DOING?" Principal Peck and Ms. Chichester were headed toward Stanley. Ms. Chichester snatched the picket fence slab from him. Stanley screamed. His hand instantly became riddled with several splinters. By this time, several other teachers had made it out into the yard to investigate the commotion.

"What's going on here?" Mr. Peck demanded . Lisa Caruso blurted out, "Stanley beat Bear with a stick." Principal Peck instantly grabbed Stanley by the back of his shirt collar.

32

"You just couldn't do as you were told...Could ya?" Stanley tried explaining his side but no reasonable adult cared or even dared to hear him out. He just watched as the other teachers consoled and nurtured Cody Washington. By now, he was use to not being heard. After all, every fight he and Salvatore had gotten into was "his fault." Any bad influence picked up by the younger siblings emanated from him or at least that was the rule. If there was so much as a crumb missing from the cookie jar, Stanley Grauso was your prime suspect. One teacher even whispered, "You little monster." Stanley just stared at her.

Stanley's senses, at that moment, heightened. He could easily hear the undertone verbiage muttered and spoken by the adults present concerning him. No one had anything good to say about Stanley Grauso.

"Go ahead...all of you...I get the shit beat out of me ...and its throw a party for the big dumb kid."

"That's it Stanley Grauso," Principal Peck shouted, "You son, are expelled from school indefinitely."

"That's the best news I heard all day." Principal Peck marched Stanley back inside. Watching Stanley go, for some was a sigh of relief but a few others actually felt sorry for him. Principal Peck had reached Mrs. Grauso. She had awakened from taking a much needed nap. The news only added more stress to her day and worry to her heart for what would become of her son. Stanley's older brother Salvatore was called down to the office and given an early dismissal to escort Stanley home. Salvatore resented Stanley and scolded him all the way home for ruining his fun on Halloween day.

★★★★★★★★★★★★★★★

Three days had passed and Alexander had just returned home from his trip with Don Ernesto. He was looking forward to an evening of chicken catchatori, a glass of wine and some good old fashioned Italian loving from Mrs. Grauso. Mrs. Grauso could always count on a frisky Alexander returning home after a few days but the stress caused by Stanley had practically ruined those plans for the evening. Mrs. Grauso was a million light years away from being in the mood and if a romantic evening meant the possibilities of another Stanley, forget about it.

Stanley stood in his father's office, with his mother, where he'd watched him for years: spying on the good, the bad and the ugly. Conversations of racketeering, boot-legging and sharlocking were second nature to him at this point. Seeing his father frustrated and upset in a disciplinary manner was almost foreign to Stanley. The scene to some degree was sort of comedic in his eyes. Mr. Grauso had been more of an older buddy toward Stanley than a father. Stanley's little chubby cheeks filled up with air from holding back his laughter. He thought to himself, "Papa's really pouring it on for Mama."

"SO YOU THINK YOUR SOME TOUGH GUY...HUH!...You get some kind of kick out of seeing your mother cry. Is that it?" Stanley shook his head.

"THEN WHAT IS IT SON?" Stanley spoke comfortably to his father.

"I want to be a hood..." For a moment, you could hear a pin drop. Mrs. Grauso stare

34

questionably in a haze: her eyes forgetting to focus, her ears forgetting to hear and her words forgetting how to formulate. Stanley's words had rocked his mother to her core. Mr. Grauso just laughed in a manner suggesting that Stanley couldn't possibly be serious.

"What the hell is this hood stuff? You wanna be like some punk at school or something?" Mr. Grauso asked.

"No Papa..." Stanley seized the moment with his infamous eye contact.

"I - want - to - be - like - Charlie...I - want -to- be - like -you." Mrs. Grauso's heart stopped. Uncontrollable gasps and breathing outward seemed the only way to survive at that moment. Deep down she believed Stanley and needed no convincing. She suddenly burst into tears. Mr. Grauso sat back thrown into utter silence, as if he were blind sided by a slug to the chest.

"Come on Papa...I know I can do it." Stanley spoke as if his request was somewhere in the norm for a ten year old. Mrs. Grauso ran over to Stanley, knelt down and grabbed him by the shoulders, shaking him profusely.

"WHAT IS THE MATTER WITH YOU?"

"I WANT TO BE A HOOD MAMA!"Out of a mother's reflex, Mrs. Grauso slapped him across the face. The strength Stanley used to brace himself felt somewhat demonic. Mrs. Grauso placed her forehead onto Stanley's and kissed him repeatedly. A small bridge of saliva mixed with tears formed on the edge of Mrs. Grauso's lips connecting to Stanley's forehead. She whispered , "Hail Mary...Mother of God...Full of

Grace..." Stanley closed his eyes for a brief moment. The turmoil caused by the stirring sound of his mother's prayers grew within him. Mr. Grauso's hand softly touched the shoulder of his wife. Her eyes opened slowly as if she had forgotten that he were in the room. He spoke softly to his wife.

"Leave us..." Mrs. Grauso clung to Stanley for dear hope. "Sweetheart please...it'll be fine...just leave us..." Alexander lifted Mrs. Grauso to her feet. Stanley would never forget the look in his mother's eyes as Mr. Grauso escorted Mrs. Grauso out of the office. Her eyes were glued to Stanley; staring at him without batting a wink, in a haze-like focus, as if something had been taken away from her. She was the vision of a soul filled with pain. Stanley's world only blackened more by his stiff and hardening heart. His way of combating any remorseful sentiments surfacing was to always focus more on his own his own selfish agendas and goals. Mr. Grauso returned to his office. He grabbed an unfinished cigarette from off of his desk, reached for his matches and relit it. The puffs he took were enormous.

"How do you know about Charlie...or should I say what do you know about me and Charlie."

The thin line between father and son disappeared altogether. Stanley reminded Alexander of things even he or *"Charlie White"* didn't want to remember: talks of judges being bribed, monies owed and monies stolen, witnessing several individuals being roughed up severely and never seeing them again afterwards, closed room conversations with honorable men from politicians, court officials and even priests, all in some way or fashion *"on the take."* Secrets embedded in the mind of his son washed ashore Alexander's dirty laundry like an ocean churning up its dirty foam. How could he have been so careless. Whether Alexander liked it or not, his son had already been a hood in the making and had himself to thank for it. Don Alexander listened as his son poured his heart out. A window of silence settled between the two once Stanley ran out of words. Mr. Grauso spoke soft but increasingly stern.

"Come here..." Stanley hesitated. Mr. Grauso extended his hand speaking in the same manner toward his son.

"I said come here..." Stanley walked over to his father.

"Look at me." Mr. Grauso said. Stanley buried his eyes deep into his father's eyes. Mr. Grauso placed both hands onto the side of Stanley's head covering his ears then kissed Stanley on both cheeks. Stanley didn't know what to make of his father's gesture, only that this was how he and others like Don Ernesto greeted one another. Nothing else was said except "good night."

****

Salvatore got up for school the next morning. His feet touched the cold wooden floor as he called out in his normal morning whisper, "Stanley get your ass up." Stanley remained dead asleep. A third bed had now been added to the spacious room shared by Salvatore and Stanley. Salvatore looked over at his little brother Freddy, now five years old, snuggled up in a ball. Salvatore walked over and tickled his little brother. Freddy turned over spilling with uncontrollable laughter.

"Say uncle." Salvatore replied. When Freddy had enough, he screamed, "Uncle." Stanley seemed to sleep right through all of the morning noise made by Salvatore and Freddy.

"Stanley you had better get your ass up before mother comes in here." Freddy mimicked Salvatore's choice of words toward Stanley.

"Get you ass up Stanley." Salvatore laughed. He whispered into Freddy's ear, this time pointing over at Stanley. Freddy got up, walked over to Stanley, with an open hand , and plastered one onto his naked back. "*SMACK!*" Stanley jumped out of his sleep.

"OUCH!..." Freddy ran behind Salvatore to avoid being hit by Stanley. Salvatore was quite affectionate and protective concerning Freddy. One would guess it had come from the constant reminder from Mrs. Grauso heard by Salvatore everyday.

"Don't let anything happen to your little brother Salvatore...and you are to let me know if Stanley does anything to him..." Stanley reached behind Salvatore trying to grab hold of a squirming Freddy.

"Get cha' panties out of a bunch Stanley! Besides, I told him to do it so if you wanna hit somebody then you gotta hit me." Stanley backed off as he'd always did in times past concerning his older brother.

"One of these days..." He said pointing his fist toward Salvatore. Salvatore responded,

"Then why not today?"

Mrs. Grauso entered the room. Her hair was a complete mess. It was evident that the swelling and puffiness around her eyes was due to excessive crying.

"What's going on in hear?" Salvatore could easily see that she was not herself this morning and as far as he was concerned, it was Stanley's fault.

Upon seeing his mother, Stanley looked the other way in an apparent shame, avoiding eye contact. Mrs. Grauso took Freddy by the hand. Stanley continued starring down at the floor dressed in nothing more than a pair of white briefs while Salvatore continued getting dressed for school.

"And why aren't you getting dressed for school young man..." Mrs. Grauso spoke stern and angrily. Stanley muttered, "I can't go back to school...that's what Mr. Peck said."

"I don't care what Principal Peck says. Your father will go down today to speak with the school's superintendent and you will go to school and stop this foolishness Stanley Grauso. Is that understood?" Stanley shouted interrupting his mother. "I TOLD YOU, I DON'T WANT TO GO TO SCHOOL!...EVER AGAIN!" Mrs. Grauso shouted back in return. Her voice thundered over Stanley's.

"I AM THE MOTHER AND YOU WILL DO AS I SAY...OR YOU WILL NOT LIVE IN MY HOUSE. NOW YOU ARE GOING TO SCHOOL AND THAT IS FINAL!" Mrs. Grauso left Stanley's room and slammed the door. The door flung back open from the force of the slam. A dripping Mr. Grauso came storming out of the bathroom wrapped in a towel. His morning shower had been interrupted.

"What's all the noise about?" He asked. Stanley shrugged his shoulders in a nonchalant fashion as if to say no big deal. Salvatore replied, "Mama's mad at Stanley again..." Mr. Grauso took a deep breath. Salvatore made his way downstairs to help Mrs. Grauso.

"Hang out up here while I go and talk to your mother..." Stanley nodded. Mr. Grauso sported a smile, then winked at Stanley.

Mr. Grauso made his way downstairs while tying his robe. After giving Rose and Dolly a kiss, he leaned in to kiss Mrs. Grauso. Mrs. Grauso leaned backward avoiding Mr. Grauso's kiss. While staring coldly at the floor, she asked, "Why aren't you bringing him back to school -- where he belongs." Mr. Grauso leaned back onto the kitchen counter, shrugged his shoulders and in a dismissive manner replied, "He doesn't want to go..."

"Just like that...Huh Alex? He doesn't want to go...You say it as if he's some child who doesn't want to eat his vegetables or something like that." Mrs. Grauso sucked in her stomach, deepened her voice and hardened her Italian accent as to mock her husband.

"So son you don't want your vegetables? Okay don't eat them and while you're at it...forget all about school...forget about life...forget all about..." Alexander blared, slapping the counter, "ALRIGHT JOSEPHINE...KNOCK IT OFF!" Mrs. Grauso stood her grounds.

"I WILL NOT KNOCK IT OFF!" By this time tempers were flaring and it was the first time the children had ever heard Mrs. Grauso contend with their father. Freddy and the girls appeared somewhat frightened. Salvatore instructed his sisters and Freddy all to get their coats. While Alexander and Josephine began drawing contentious words, both, from the English and Italian vocabulary, Salvatore quietly left for school with his younger siblings.

"WHAT DO YOU WANT ME TO DO?" Alexander shouted. "HE DOESN'T WANT TO GO!"

"WHAT DO YOU MEAN, WHAT DO I WANT YOU TO DO? YOU'RE A MAN...AND YOU ARE HIS FATHER! IT IS YOUR JOB TO MAKE HIM GO, ALEX!" Mr. Grauso calmed down for a moment containing his own frustrations. Deep down he knew Mrs. Grauso was right. Either that, or a screaming Mrs. Grauso scared him just as much as it did the children. His tone now became more reasoning.

"So I make him go...and he'll just go right back to being Stanley again and again and again..."

"So beat his ass..." Alexander flung his hand toward his wife, clearly brushing off her suggestion.

"Ah... Josephine, that stuff doesn't work." Mr. Grauso stood in Mrs. Grauso's way. He softly placed his hands onto her shoulders. Mrs. Grauso attempted to pull away from her husband but appeared too weak to do so. He pleaded with her softly, "Josephine don't do this..."

41

"Alex you know what happens to kids like Stanley who go on to do this kind of thing. I can't see that for my son."

"He's my son too Josephine." Mrs. Grauso's head rested on her husband's shoulder.

"We always talked about Salvatore becoming a doctor and Stanley, a lawyer or something...anything but a hood."

"Then maybe you should've married a doctor or a lawyer..."

"What's that suppose to mean, Alex?"

"It means that our children don't walk around everyday watching doctors and lawyers."

"But they see you work everyday with the courts and how respected you are..." Mr. Grauso interrupted, "No my dear...I'm afraid Stanley has seen a whole lot more." Mrs. Grauso opened her mouth to speak but Alexander placed his finger over her lips in a soft loving manner.

"I am afraid that this is our doing as much as it is Stanley's, Josephine...We can't just blame Stanley."

"Alex, what you do is what you do. I have been a good mother and..." Mr. Grauso interrupted, "...And you know we do not live the way that we do on what I make as an interpreter at the courts alone. You pretend not to see because that is what most wives choose to do." At that moment Stanley walked in. Mrs. Grauso's eyes rolled her son's way. It was hard to tell what upset Mrs. Grauso more; the fact that Stanley wasn't returning to school or his cold dismissive attitude toward her as if he hadn't done anything wrong.

Stanley walked over to a plate of untouched pancakes and sausage located on the stove. He picked up a cold sausage link but before he could get it into his mouth, Mrs. Grauso slapped the sausage clean out of Stanley's hand.

"You want to be a man? A man makes his own food?"

"What you do that for?" Stanley shouted. Mrs. Grauso grabbed the plate of food from off of the stove and threw it clean into the garbage.

"I will not feed a hood," she shouted. Mr. Grauso pleaded with his wife.

"Josephine be reasonable." In a disrespectful retort Stanley blurted out, "Then how come you feed Papa...he's a hood...and a good one." Mrs. Grauso instantly reached into a kitchen drawer and pulled out a long wooden spoon. She lunged toward Stanley but Mr. Grauso stepped in creating a barrier between she and Stanley.

"Go to your room Stanley until your mother and I finish talking. Is that understood?"

"But I'm hungry," Stanley shouted in a whining manner.

"Well then I guess you should've gotten up for school and you would've eaten then...So now I tell you when to eat. Now go..." Stanley stomped away with each step growing louder than the previous one. Mr. Grauso sat down at the kitchen table. The strain in his eyes made it obvious that this whole thing with Stanley was starting to take its toll on him Mrs. Grauso could see the wear and tear on her husband's countenance.

Mrs. Grauso caved in from the desires of being cold and wanting to argue. Mr. Grauso motioned for her to sit on his lap. She easily took him up on his offer. The two shared a passionate kiss. Their smile and bedroom eyes insinuated a much needed appointment in the bedroom. Mrs. Grauso's head lay flush on Mr. Grauso's head. She rubbed his shoulders while he stroked her back, occasionally palming her backside.

"What are we going to do Alex?"

"He can't go back Josephine...he just can't." Mr. Grauso's hand gripped Mrs. Grauso's backside even more. "Think about...if this keeps up, it will ultimately have an affect on Salvatore and the girls' education and that, sweetheart, isn't fair. It would be like punishing them for wanting good. Stanley is our responsibility and our child not Salvatore's and the girls." Mrs. Grauso stared off into a blank stare. The thought of giving up on Stanley seemed to much to bear. Although any mother would've probably thrown in the towel long ago, *"any mother"* wasn't Stanley's mother; she was.

"He'll be fine,"said Mr. Grauso. "And someday, he'll have to live with the decisions he's made. Until then I'll keep him with me at all times."

"Maybe he should stay with me sometimes." Mrs. Grauso suggested.

"No Josephine...He wants to be a man and he must learn to hold his own like a man. Staying with you will only make him soft and a good cook." Mrs. Grauso smiled.

"Leave him to me...you'll see...he'll be begging to go back to school." Mrs. Grauso clenched her husband around the neck and kissed him . Her lips kissed from the back of

44

his ear all the way down to the coast of his neck. His morning manly scent aroused her the more.

"Enough about Stanley...I think I want to go and lay down." She said in a soft spoken and seductive tone.

"Is that right?...Well I think I want to go and lay down also." The two slowly journeyed upstairs kissing and caressing in between steps. Stanley heard them coming so he jumped back into his bed and pretended to be sound asleep . Mr. And Mrs. Grauso peeped in on their ten year old juvenile clutter. Although in a world of trouble, something about Stanley still made his parents smile. Mr. Grauso walked into his bedroom. Sitting on the mahogany bureau was an old phonograph record player used to play George Gershwin and other classics to drown out occasional love making whenever the kids were home. Swanee River began to play. Mrs. Grauso shut their door and it was off to the races. Stanley laid in his bed thinking, "They sure listen to this song a lot."

CHAPTER FIVE

$\mathbf{F}$ive years had passed. The year was now 1927 and talks or chances of Stanley ever returning to school had only shown signs of abating. Mrs. Grauso revisited the subject several times throughout the years but by now it had only become a welshing argument. Mr. Grauso's patented contemptuous sneer and stern tone always seemed to stop Mrs. Grauso three words into any discussion on the matter.

"Can't beat a dead horse, Josephine," he'd always say. Mrs. Grauso had no problem in making her attitude known. She had a way of sighing and folding her hands before stomping off and muttering under her breath, "It's not a horse, it's our child." Mr. Grauso would simply smile as Josephine walked away.

Mr. Grauso had found a way of emancipating Stanley from the school system through the courts. The agreement was contingent upon certain criteria being met by Stanley at

Mr. Grauso's discretion. The school's superintendant, including several teachers within the district, were certainly not fans of Stanley's. And since Mr. Grauso or Mrs. Grauso never really pushed the issue, neither did the school system. As a result of their negligence and lack of stern discipline, Stanley Grauso was given a free pass to slip through the educational crack. So to keep peace, Stanley spent most of his days with Mr. Grauso. Alexander always tried to reassure Mrs. Grauso that he was considerate of the people and places he'd taken Stanley. But a mother's intuition along with Stanley's occasional slip of the tongue and behavior always told her differently. The other children, however, showed signs of promise and aspiration.

There was something strange about the relationship developing between Stanley and his father. Alexander seemed to take a more stern approach in demanding a more mature attitude from a fifteen year old but Stanley's witty personality seemed to bring out the kid in Alexander. The more Stanley watched his father rise in both power and in favor within the Connecticut underworld circles, the more he became drawn like a magnet in striving for the same. Even while learning the ropes from his father, Stanley plotted, anxiously waiting for the day in which he would venture out on his own.

Alexander had become quite comfortable escorting his new sidekick and partner in crime around town. Stanley had memorized all of the rules: how to gamble, when to talk, when not to talk, when to hang around and when to split. There were several clients in whom Alexander trusted his son to collect certain monies due to him as a result of loan

47

shark payments.

Alexander had mapped out his own terms in working with Don Ernesto without joining his organization altogether in addition to running his own rackets and keeping up with the courts. The two had become like brothers. Don Ernesto loved Alexander because of his ingenious style of book keeping. On paper, Don Ernesto looked like a flourishing entrepreneur. In reality, the majority of criminals and prostitutes bailed out of jail in those days belonged to Mr. Ernesto and were passed through the system using Alexander's wit and several owed favors in connection with his bail bondsman business. Very few criminals ever saw so much as a day in court because of Alexander's reach. Don Ernesto owed Alexander Grauso big time for the heat kept off of him due to Mr. Grauso's efforts. Whether jokingly over a glass of wine or casually in keeping with business, Alexander Grauso reminded Don Ernesto as often as he could. Alexander Grauso had become what no man in his circles had become: a pivotal pinpoint of synergy and communication between the justice world and the criminal world combined.

One Sunday morning, Stanley sat in Mr. Grauso's office reading the *New York Times* newspaper. The newspaper at that time was only two-cents and purchased by Mr. Grauso regularly. Stanley loved how reading the paper made his father look. It seemed to enhance his ingenious swagger even more. He too made it a practice to read the *New York Times* on a regular basis. Stanley's reading skills improved over the years as a result. His spelling skills did not improve.

Mrs. Grauso's operatic voice could be heard squealing through the house as she called out to her husband, "Alex..."

"Yeah!" He replied. An all dolled up Mrs. Grauso came into the office. Mr. Grauso let out a huge cat whistle. Stanley laughed, placing his fingers into both ears.

"Oh Alex, stop it...", she said with a smile.

"Can't a man compliment his wife?" Mr. Grauso looked over and winked at Stanley.

"Then say, 'sweetheart, don't you look ravishing'. A whistle is not a compliment for a lady."

"Oh no, then what is it?"

"It's nothing more than a cheap mating call for a woman who doesn't respect herself..."

"Well in that case, sweetheart , don't you look *ravishing!*" Mrs. Grauso smiled.

"Why thank you." Mrs. Grauso continued, "I'm taking the kids to morning mass. Salvatore is over at a friend's house. I need money for offering and I have to pick up a few things from the grocery store. Oh...and I have to pay Mr. Goldstein for the girls' dresses." Mr. Goldstein was a well known tailor from the community. At that moment Freddy, Theresa and Rose walked in. Freddy looked quite debonair in his three piece knickerbocker suit and *Florsheim* shoes. Theresa and Rose both wore beautiful floral and

49

laced pattern dresses. Mr. Grauso smiled.

"Well what do you think the priest is going to say when he sees two angels from heaven visiting his church? Mr. Grauso took both girls into his arms and kissed them.

"The two of you look wonderful." Freddy approached Mr. Grauso.

"What about me Papa?"

"A gentleman's gentleman and a chip off of the old block: just like your old man kid." Mr. Grauso went into his pocket and gave each of the children a quarter. He then opened up his wallet to Mrs. Grauso.

"Take what you need." Mrs. Grauso reached in taking over fifty dollars. Mr. Grauso jokingly complained, "Come on Josephine, a couple of dresses and some food can't be that expensive."

"We also have to give offering today Alex."

"Offering!....And what is God going to give us?"

"Alex stop it...that's blasphemy." Mrs. Grauso kissed Mr. Grauso then kissed Stanley affectionately on his forehead. The look on Stanley's face appeared, to some extent, undeserving of his mother's kiss.

"Mama will see you later okay?"

"Yes Mama." He replied. Mr. Grauso suggested that she take Stanley along.

"He's all yours," she said with a smile while exiting with the other children. For a moment Stanley appeared saddened by his mother's comment.

"Suck it up kid." Mr. Grauso stated.

"Suck what up?"

"Never mind..." said Mr. Grauso, "So I guess it's just you and me today." Stanley nodded.

"Look Stanley, I'm going to take you out and show you a few things today."

"What kind of things Papa?"

"I want you to know all of the ins and outs of the business. It's important that all of the important people who know me, know you too. If anything should ever happen to me, you'll still be able to help the family. Got me?" Stanley nodded.

Mr. Grauso rose from his desk. Stanley watched as his father made his way over to a small corner of his office. Several large boxes were stacked in front of a closed door. As far as Stanley could remember, the door had always remained shut with the stack of boxes blocking its way. Mr. Grauso moved the boxes from in front of the door then pulled a set of keys from his right pant's pocket. He sorted through the key ring of approximately ten

51

to twelve keys.

"You see this key?" Stanley nodded nonchalantly.

"Get over here, where you can see it good." Stanley moved in closer, tripping over the boxes as he made his way over to his father.

"Now do you see it?" Mr. Grauso said, shaking the keys as if Stanley were deaf.

"Yes Papa! I told you I saw it before." Mr. Grauso handed Stanley the key.

"Open that door." Stanley took the keys from his father's hand and opened the door slowly. On the other side was a stairwell leading to the upstairs where Mr. Grauso housed other offices and sometimes where others, including immigrants occasionally worked for him. Mr. Grauso walked up approximately four steps.

"Not even your mother knows about this. You got me?"

"Yes Papa." Mr. Grauso motioned for Stanley to join him on the small stairwell. As Stanley stood next to his father, Mr. Grauso reached over and closed the door. The stairwell became darkened. Mr. Grauso blindly felt his way around the wall space behind the closed door for the light switch.

After a split second of fumbling, Mr. Grauso hit the switch. He then pointed downward at the wall space once covered by the opened door.

"What is that?" Stanley exclaimed.

"That my friend is our little secret," said Mr. Grauso. Located on the lower part of the wall was a panel covering the doorway to a small crawl space. Mr. Grauso removed the panel clearing the way to an open space.

"Wow." Stanley whispered. "A SAFE!" Mr. Grauso reached over, repeating the combination as he turned the knob on its door.

"Thirty eight left - fifteen right - then two full turns to thirty two left. You got that? Repeat it." Stanley repeated, "Thirty eight left - fifteen right - then two full turns to thirty two left." Mr. Grauso smiled.

"Good boy..." The door swung open slowly. Stanley's eyes shot open as a small field mouse ran past the opened safe door. But it wasn't the field mouse that caught his attention. Several large stacks of one-hundred dollar bills wrapped in bands by the ten-thousands lay in the belly of the large safe. Stanley bent over and reached in.

"How deep does this thing go Papa and how much money is in here?" Sitting on top of several stacks of money were a few pieces of fine jewelry that belonged to Mr. Grauso: a pinky ring made of solid gold containing a huge diamond center stone and a fancy gold watch. Stanley placed the watch around his left wrist and the pinky ring onto his left hand. Mr. Grauso laughed as Stanley flaunted his wrist and pinky in the air.

"What are these Papa?" He said placing his hand on several legal size envelopes also wedged between several stacks of money.

"These are....what we like to call favors owed."

"And why is that?" Stanley asked. Mr. Grauso pulled one of the envelopes from the safe and opened it. He removed several of its documents. The documents were foreign to Stanley but he knew that they were of great significance because of the seal placed on each one. "These, my son, are immigration papers. Some have been approved and some are waiting approval."

"So why do you call them favors?" Stanley asked.

"These papers have helped a lot of people come into this country for a better chance. You know, at the so-called *American dream*." Stanley's expression became more inquisitive at that moment. Mr. Grauso continued.

"As a result of our helping people, many who's names appear on these papers have gone on to become quite successful in many ways: good jobs, high ranking positions, their own businesses. Those people in turn, help us get things done that under normal circumstances, couldn't get done. It gives us what I like to call...REACH. Understand?"

"Yeah...you wash their hands and they owe you big time when it comes to washing yours."

"EXACTLY!" Mr. Grauso exclaimed with a smile.

"So why do we have them here...why don't they have them?" Stanley asked.

"We give them copies but the originals stay with us until they have paid the debt in favors or some form of work. It keeps a certain amount of loyalty on the table when doing business." Mr. Grauso paused for a brief moment.

"Look at me Stanley..." Stanley's eyes fastened onto his father's eyes. Mr. Grauso stared deeply into his son's eyes.

"There is nothing more important to me than loyalty...The same should be for you."

"Yes Papa." Both smiled at each other.

"Now take off my watch and ring and let us be going. Time to live a little." As Stanley removed the ring and watch from his person he noticed a cherry wood handle sticking out from behind one of the envelopes. The make and model of the gun wasn't clear. His heart fluttered like butterfly wings. It was the first time he'd actually seen a real gun. Curiosity and a hint of excitement stirred within him. Mr. Grauso's eyes traced the pathway leading from Stanley's eyes into the safe. It was obvious that his fixation was with the neatly polished handle belonging to his forty five hand revolver. Stanley slowly reached into the safe. His efforts were stopped however when Mr. Grauso grabbed him by the wrist.

"Come on...lets go," he said, interrupting Stanley's wet dream with the forty five revolver. Stanley then placed the watch and ring back into the safe where they belonged. Mr. Grauso closed the envelope containing several immigration documents and placed them back into the safe as well. He then pulled a wrapped stack of cash from the safe and placed it in the left inside pocket of his suit jacket. Stanley's eyes followed the cash until it reached its destination. The yellow and white band wrapped around the money read clearly, *Ten-Thousand Dollars*. Mr. Grauso then closed the safe door, securing it shut. "Always turn the knob like this to make sure it locks. Got me?" Stanley watched as his dad carefully spun the knob on the safe, pulling on the door, making sure that it was shut properly.

The two then exited the narrow stairwell into the office. Stanley locked the door on the outside with the keys Mr. Grauso had given him, then placed the boxes back in front of the door as they were before.

"So what's all the money in your pocket for?" Stanley asked.

"It's a surprise. Time to live a little." Mr. Grauso walked out of the home with Stanley following behind. The two approached an early compact Ford Model-T sitting in the driveway.

Stanley hopped in and closed the door. The car appeared to be in poor condition and on its last leg. It took Mr. Grauso approximately eight minutes to get the car to properly idle and started. Stanley instantly became nauseous with all of the backfiring and permeating fumes coming from the car.

"I don't feel so good..." he exclaimed. Mr. Grauso patted Stanley on the back.

"It'll go away once we start rolling. The fresh air will clear it all out...." Mr. Grauso pulled out of the driveway and proceeded up the street. Stanley sat in the passenger seat holding his stomach while nodding like a drunken sailor.

After about a ten minute drive, Mr. Grauso had driven the jumping jalopy onto Sydney street, located on the Northeastern side of Seaside Park in Bridgeport CT. He immediately made a quick right, pulling into the driveway of a place known as THE LOCOMOBILE CO. Several new cars, different makes and models, all sat outside on display.

"Wow!" Stanley exclaimed, "Are we getting a new car Papa?"

"You betcha' kid."

"Which one is ours?"

"Ours should be inside...It's being customized."

"Customized? What's that?"

"That's when they give you a bunch of fancy stuff so you can say that you car's better than anyone else's."

"I'll be old enough to drive soon Papa. Will you teach me to drive it?" Mr. Grauso nodded casually indicating that he would.

At that moment, a man could be seen coming out of the Locomobile building approaching Mr. Grauso and Stanley. He seemed to put on a smile the closer he got to their car and his features became more clear to Stanley.

"This guy is a good man to know Stanley." Alexander stepped out of the car. The two greeted each other with an embrace and a kiss to each cheek. The man referred to Alexander Grauso as *Don Alexander.*

"Don Alexander...So good to see you," he exclaimed in a warm fashion. Mr. Grauso referred to the man as Jack Cisero.

"Stanley, get out of the car. There's somebody I want you to meet." Jack Cisero extended his hand toward Stanley as he got out of the car making his way around to the two men. Stanley immediately shook hands with him.

"So, this is the little Don...?" Jack Cisero's grip was firm. Stanley's hand felt as if all of the circulation had been cut off, as if his entire arm went numb. Though moderate and generous in his tone and persona, there was something intriguingly cold about the smile and the stare in Jack's eyes-almost a light of creepiness. Stanley thought to himself while

58

letting go of the man's somewhat divisive grip, "If Papa says he's cool... then he must be..." Stanley sported a three-dollar smile while the two men continued in their dry humor toward each other.

"Come on, lets go around the back...I can't wait for you to see this thing!" Jack said to Mr. Grauso. The men started out for the back of the service building. Stanley followed as Jack Cisero continued on.

"When I saw this thing Alex, I wanted to keep it for myself...but I said Alex will kill me." Both men laughed.

"Because I myself would kill for this car." Jack Cisero stopped in his tracks and pointed his finger for Mr. Grauso to see. Mr. Grauso's jaws dropped and Stanley's eyes lit up like a Christmas tree on Christmas day.

"Is that our car." Stanley shouted.

"That, my son, is your father's car..." Jack replied.

In an open garage entrance to the service area stood a young man waxing a brand new 1925 customized Locomobile. The man smiled while daubing the rag in a small can of hand wax. The rag made a crisp popping noise, as he shook it, after putting the finishing touches on the driver's door.

"She's all yours, Mr. Cisero." said the man to his boss. Stanley immediately ran over to the car and hopped in. Mr. Cisero and Mr. Grauso approached the automobile.

"She's got all the bells and whistles you asked for Alex." Mr. Cisero opened the trunk and showed Alex the engine.

"She's the only eight cylinder in town." The black on black standard shift chrome Locomobile was a sheer beaut. Other features included were the stylish black velvet upholstery, maroon carpeted floorboards, black walled steel lined tires and other perks. Mr. Cisero handed Alexander Grauso the keys and it was off to the races. Mr. Grauso climbed into his new automobile, grinning ear to ear. His hand stroked the steering wheel with a sense of pride.

"Now this is how a Don is suppose to drive," said Jack. Stanley sat in the passenger seat looking around and staring in amazement. His hands stroked the velvet seats like a boy petting his favorite dog. His eyes stared up at the car's ceiling and then into its spacious three passenger rear. Mr. Grauso handed Jack Cisero the keys to his former car.

"Take care of that other piece of shit for me, will ya?"

"Say no more, Alex." Jack replied. Mr. Grauso reached into the right inner pocket of his blazer and pulled out the small stack of one-hundred dollar bills. Don Alexander peeled the stack in half like a dealer spliting a deck of cards at a black jack table.

"Five-thousand we said?"

"Yes. Five-thousand even." Jack Cisero replied. Alexander Grauso slipped Jack Cisero Five-thousand dollars in cash.

"I have the bill of sale with the other paperwork on my desk..." said Jack. Mr. Cisero stared at the money as if it were a naked lady before transferring it from Mr. Grauso's hand into the right inner pocket of his blazer. Alexander Grauso then peeled five one-hundred dollar bills from his small stash and handed them to Jack Cisero.

"A little something for yourself Jack..." At first, Jack refused but Alexander kept his hand extended with the money folded in it. Stanley jokingly replied, "I'll take it..." but soon afterward Jack Cisero graciously took the gift extended to him from Don Alexander.

"Meet me on the side where my office is located," said Jack while walking away into the service entrance. Alexander drove the well crafted piece of automobile machinery around the building. Jack Cisero walked out of the sales entrance and handed Mr. Grauso an envelope containing receipts and several documents.

"That's everything you need Alex...Oh, I almost forgot...the stick."

"What stick?" Asked Mr. Grauso.

"The stick to beat off all the girls that are going to come your way for a ride." Said Jack jokingly.

"Nonsense..." Alex replied with a smile.

"Oh yeah? Said Jack, "Then let me use this baby on the weekend and I'll gladly oblige them." Both men laughed, including Stanley. The men soon ceased from a small trade off of dirty jokes and said their pardons. Mr. Grauso peeled out of the parking lot feeling like a brand new man. As for Stanley, he just sat in the passenger seat in awe: every now and then, repeating, "Now this is what you call a mobster's car..." Mr. Grauso just shrugged it off with a smile and laughed.

"We're not mobsters, Stanley...we're business men." In those days *"mobster"* was a cool term of endearment amongst kids but not so well regarded by adults, especially those involved in underworld activities.

Mr. Grauso had driven around town for approximately twenty minutes. Midway stops, complete halts and cruising at moderate to immoderate speeds made it obvious that Alexander Grauso wanted to be seen in his new classic. Stanley's peering through the window and sticking his head out shouting to a few friends, "CHECK OUT THE NEW WHEELS," didn't help much either; complete show-offs.

"So where are we going now Papa...?" Stanley asked.

Alexander soon made his way into what was known then as the prestigious Brooklawn area, located in Fairfield Connecticut. Mr. Grauso came to a huge colonial villa estate home set in front of a mile long beautifully landscaped driveway. Stanley's jaws dropped. The immaculate home was set on what appeared to be approximately a hundred acres of level and wooded land. The floral landscape looked like a harmonious oil painting with several pieces of sunlight cascading on each flower. Several expensive classic automobiles graced the property, all with a waxed shine that could easily blind anyone. A 1924 Studebaker, Rolls Royce Silver Ghost, and Pierce-Arrow, to name a few, were their makes and models. Stanley wondered if any of the cars were ever driven . The tires with their white walls and black tread looked clean enough to eat from. What appeared to be a separate in-law quarters and a couple of warehouses sat at a distance from the main house on the well manicured land front. Alexander pulled his car around to the back of the house.

"Who's house is this, Papa?" Before Mr. Grauso could answer Stanley's question, a well dressed middle-aged man, holding a glass of wine walked out onto the terrace to greet Alexander. Stanley recognized the man. It was Don Ernesto Cozza. Most of the time Stanley had seen him, he was at a distance or sitting down but today the well dressed, short, buffed man he had spent years spying on was up close and personal.

"Check out the wheels!" He shouted as he approached Mr. Grauso's new car. Ernie Cozza noticed Stanley.

"Who is this Alex...This can't be the little guy?"

"Yeah, Ernie, that's Stanley." Alex replied. Ernie joked with Stanley, "How's the right hand kid? Still pack a mean one?" Stanley nodded while holding his right fist in the

63

air.

"Get out of the car and let me take a good look at you kid?" Said Ernie. Mr. Grauso

nudged Stanley to get out of the car. Stanley opened the door and stepped out of the car.

Ernie Cozza grabbed him by the face and kissed him on both cheeks.

"I use to love the stories your father would tell me about you kid..You got a lot of

heart," he said with each hand pressed upon Stanley's arms. Like Jack Cisero from the car

lot, Mr. Cozza, up close, gave Stanley the willies. Stanley made it a practice however, of

never showing anyone that he was even the slightest bit intimidated. He'd never forgotten

the rule of eye contact concerning business, taught to him by Mrs. O'Neal. In addition

there was the rule and motto pressed upon him by his father: Always lock eyes and never

be the first to look away unless the other party looks away.

There was something about the short, stout, legitimate gangster that seemed to

impress Stanley.

"I really like your place...and your cars..." said Stanley.

"Can you drive kid?" Ernie Cozza yelled out before Stanley could answer.

"HEY POPEYE! Bring me my keys." Stanley spoke nervously, "I can't drive Sir..."

"Too bad...I was gonna let you drive anyone you wanted." Ernie Cozza looked at

Alexander and jokingly uttered, "Hey, let the kid have some fun. Teach him to drive for goodness sake."

"How's about it Papa." Stanley gestured.

"What can I say, you both got me cornered..." Mr. Grauso jested. At that moment a tall, muscular, squint-eye man wearing a button up shirt who's sleeves were rolled just above his massive forearms walked out. It was apparent by the way he greeted Mr. Grauso that the two were very familiar with one another.

"Here you go boss," he said handing Ernie Cozza several keys to the classic automobiles stationed around the home. The man stood about a foot taller than Ernie with a shoulder span that spread out like a hawk. Ernie refused.

"Never mind...Would you believe it? The kid can't drive." Stanley seemed taken back a bit by the man's size.

"Don't worry son...he won't bite," said Mr. Grauso. Ernie Cozza jokingly interrupted, "he won't bite you...but believe me kid...HE BITES!" At that moment all of the men including Stanley laughed. Even though Ernie Cozza's gesture made light of the moment, Stanley knew by the snarling glare in Ernie Cozza and his father's eyes that there was some serious truth to what Ernie had spoken concerning the massive brick house of humanity standing before him. Each one of them seem to reminisce of a memory or two that could easily confirm Mr. Cozza's statement. The man extended his hand

65

toward Stanley.

"Popeye's the name. I'm Mr. Cozza's bodyguard..." Stanley shook hands with Popeye and even though looking up seemed like it was breaking his neck, eye contact was made indefinitely. Stanley introduced himself.

"I'm Stanley..."Mr. Grauso reached into the car and pulled out a briefcase. He and Ernie seemed to engage in a conversation concerning business. The two men walked off to the side as Stanley continued talking with Popeye.

"So you can't drive, huh kid? That's too bad. Mr. Cozza would've given you the keys to any one of them."

"Yeah, I know...but I'll learn quick. My Dad's gonna teach me." Popeye then suggested, "And if your old man doesn't mind... I can even show you a thing or two behind the wheel also."

"Really?" Stanley was very excited by now. Popeye didn't seem as ferocious after all.

"Just tell him to drop you off sometimes..." Stanley was all in.

"So what do you like? What can you do?" Asked Popeye.

"I can play cards...pretty good," Stanley's answered. Popeye looked at Stanley like a mouse gazing at a piece of cheese.

"Got any money?" he said muttering while pulling a deck of cards half way out of his right pants pocket for Stanley to see. Stanley smiled.

"Hey Papa...Got any money? Popeye and I are gonna play cards while you and Mr. Cozza talk business." Mr. Grauso handed Stanley a crisp one-hundred dollar bill. Popeye's eyes widened, accompanied by a devilish grin.

"Hey Popeye...If this kid's anything like his old man, watch out...He'll take your pay check," Ernie Cozza jested. Mr. Grauso winked at Stanley.

"He stinks at playing cards...but let him have some fun...right Stanley?" Stanley smiled winking back at his father. Mr. Grauso looked at Popeye tapping his briefcase lightly.

"Go easy on him Popeye...you just remember, I got your paycheck here in my briefcase."

"And don't gamble the last dime away, Stanley." Stanley replied, "I wont..." as he and Popeye journeyed over to one of Ernie Cozza's warehouses stationed on the massive property at a distance from the main house. Alexander and Ernie both walked into Ernie's home.

"That's quite a kid you got there Alex." Ernie stated.
The two men were greeted by Ernie Cozza's personal chef upon entering Mr. Cozza's

spacious kitchen. Ernie walked over to the sink, washed his hands and cut into a freshly baked apple pie sitting on the counter. Two huge slices were cut by Mr. Cozza. He insisted that Alex join him.

"My goodness Alex...you gotta try this... Tastes just like my mother's pie from Italy." Mr. Grauso was no stranger to Ernie's kitchen. He knew exactly which drawer contained the silverware. By the time Alex walked over to the drawer and grabbed two forks , Ernie had already begun putting the smack down on his piece of pie. Apple filling and small pieces of crust trickled down Ernie's hand, onto the sleeve of his shirt and then onto the kitchen floor.

"Stop being a pig...will ya?" Alexander said jokingly. "You're getting pie all over the fucking place." Ernie just laughed.

"If I want to take the pie: shit in it and make a mess...it's mine to do. What's it to ya?" Both men laughed hysterically. Alexander's laughter was uncontrollable while staring at his friend.

"You're something else. You know that?" Ernie just smiled.

Alexander Grauso was one of very few men whom Ernie Cozza allowed himself to loosen up around. It was said that Ernie Cozza only had emotions for very few: his parents and his close friend, Alexander Grauso.

Both men finished their pie and journeyed to Ernie's living room. The room was spacious and immaculate and smelled like new furniture. A huge oil painting of Ernie's

68

parents hung over the fireplace in a beautifully handcrafted gold frame.

"I always love looking at that painting," said Alexander. The two men plopped down onto Ernie's exquisite Italian furniture.

"Let's get right down to it, Ernie: You're going to have to start stashing a lot of the money from the cat houses. It's starting to become a little too much. Pretty soon the IRS could audit you...start bringing your payroll and even your legitimate businesses into question...know what I mean?" Don Ernesto replied, "I thought too much money was a good thing. The more we make, the more they're allowed to take. Right?" Alexander Grauso leaned forward making eye contact with Ernie. His stare showed a deep concern, almost like a doctor ready to address his patient.

Alexander grabbed a small gold-plated lion like figurine from the coffee table in front of him. "Look Ernie, if we we're selling these or pretending to sell these, our books and inventory would have to show to some degree that we're in the business of selling them or at least having enough on hand to justify being in that type of business. The illusion has to not only look real but feel real too."

"So what's your point? We just buy whatever we need, right?"

"It's not that easy Ernie. The cat houses are listed as real estate properties and have been for a while. So the income has to line up with having or running rental properties. These houses are making money hand over fist. More than the numbers rackets and almost just as much as the booze on some occasions."

Don Ernesto interrupted, "So we buy more properties."

"No Ernie," Alexander replied. "If anything - I say we close a couple of them down.

Especially the one on Gilbert street." Don Ernesto immediately began shaking his head in

total disagreement. Alexander pleaded with his friend, "Come on Ernie. I've always

told you, the tiniest spark can cause the biggest fires and the biggest fires bring the most

attention. There's a lot of smoke coming from these houses and it's best to put the spark

out now before the fire spreads." Don Ernesto's look remained stern. It was clear that he

and Alexander were not going to see eye to eye on the issues with Don Ernesto's cat

houses. He walked over to the fireplace. His back remained turned toward

Alexander as he gazed up at the oil painting of his parents. Alexander stared at the picture

as well. Don Ernesto's father's ghostly image seemed to breathe on its own while staring

back at him.

"What else can we do?" asked Don Ernesto. "I mean, think about it, Alex. Surely

there's something you can do to legitimize the extra money coming in. We've got just

about every politician in our pocket...hell, they're part of the reason the cat houses stay

so busy."

"Not without sending up a bunch of red flags and jeopardizing the other businesses. I

don't trust those fucking guys Ernie. And you've got to understand, heat on you means

heat on me. You're going to have to hide a great deal of that money...in a hole...in a safe...a

bag or something."

70

Don Ernesto turned to his friend, "The thing about hiding is that someone eventually steals from you. The risk of someone knowing and then telling. Whispers turn to rumors and then all of your enemies become thieves in the night. You know how this shit works Alex."

"This place is secured like Fort Knox. Who could possibly get in here...with your men? Forget about it." Alexander replied.

"It's not me worrying whether or not anyone can make it in. There's plenty of land to bury their asses out back...but who needs the added stress and extra headaches Alexander? ...Who needs it?" Alexander walked over to the fireplace and stood on Don Ernesto's left.

"Then close the damn things down, Ernie," he whispered. Don Ernesto's eyes remained fixed on his parents' antique image and with a soft tone he turned to Alexander and whispered. "Can't do that Alex." Alexander Grauso walked away from the fireplace throwing both hands in the air.

"I don't get it. I just don't get it. You've never not taken my advice before, Ernie."

"And you've never asked me to just turn down or throw away enormous amounts of money Alexander..."

"Come on Ernie, you already have enormous amounts of money. You're sitting on a gold mine. What more could you want? How much more could you possibly need?"

"You wouldn't understand Alex. My entire family in Italy depends on me. My brother Frank, everyone here, they all depend on me and me alone. I swear, sometimes it's worse than having kids and a family." Alexander just laughed. Don Ernesto grabbed the scotch bottle from the mantle and poured himself a glass of scotch.

"Look... lets just leave the cat houses to me. Okay?" Alexander just shook his head. It was apparent that he wasn't getting through to his friend. Both men remained silent for about thirty seconds. Don Ernesto served Alexander a glass of scotch. Alexander starred at Ernie holding the glass of scotch.

"Go on...take it," Ernie said wearing a smirk. Alexander stared into the radiance of the scotch as it mingled with the rooms sunlight. Smiling in return, he gently took the glass out of Ernie's hand.

"You do know if you were anyone else..."

"Yeah...I know Alexander. You'd tell me where to go and where I can shove my money. But I'm not just anybody else. We are like brothers...and brothers just don't walk out on each other." Alexander downed the glass of scotch in one swig. His mouth remained tightly shut gritting his teeth from the heat of the home made grade "A" whiskey.

Meanwhile, approximately two hours had passed. Stanley, Popeye and some of Ernie's other boys all sat around the card table playing a game of stud poker: five cards open hand. Stanley was smashing them. His One-Hundred Dollar bank had now increased into Three-Hundred and Fifty Dollars. Popeye blurted out, "I swear if you weren't Don

72

Alexander's kid, I'd take you back in the quarry and give you a good reason to give us our money back."

"Oh yeah...and what reason would that be?" said Stanley while watching Popeye through corner of his eye.

"Your life kid...that a good enough reason?" All of the other guys sitting at the table burst into an uproar of laughter. Stanley remained poised, chuckling a little himself while dealing the last hand then said to Popeye, "and how about if you weren't Mr. Ernie's boy I'd knock ya fucking teeth out of your mouth and watch them hit the ground like a set of loose dice." For about five seconds silence hung in the air. All of a sudden Popeye burst out laughing. It wasn't long before the laughter turned into a domino effect with the other guys joining in.

"I like you kid...you gotta' lot of heart," said Popeye to Stanley. Stanley threw the last card. Popeye's compliment of swelling words seemed to fill Stanley's heart with pride. Stanley reached down by the back leg of his chair and grabbed a glass sitting on the floor. The glass was half way filled with log cabin boot legged whiskey. Some of the ice were melted and the color of the whiskey appeared to settle at the bottom of the glass. Stanley kept the glass on the floor to avoid being caught drinking in case his father came into the room where he and the boys were playing. After crushing the guys in another hand of stud poker, Popeye and the boys folded, bowing out gracefully. Stanley's earnings were now a little over four-hundred dollars. Popeye looked out of the window.

He could spot Alexander Grauso walking toward the building just a short distance from the main house.

"Hey kid, here comes your old man," he said to Stanley. Stanley instantly slid his whiskey glass over to one of the guys.

"Here this belongs to you..." Popeye quickly reached into his pocket and slid Stanley a piece of peppermint candy. Stanley quickly began gathering up his winnings.

"Why such long looks on your faces girls?" Stanley began counting his earnings, separating some of the cash. Mr. Grauso entered the small warehouse. Stanley stood over the table talking smack to Ernie's monstrous goons.

"The next time I won't be so nice. Got me?" By the time Mr. Grauso had made it over to the table, Stanley had given each of the men twenty-five dollars of their money back. Stanley made no apologies about throwing the money onto the table in an arrogant fashion for each of the guys to scoop up. Mr. Grauso smiled watching the men scrounge the table, each reaching desperately for his share.

"So I see you guys have gotten to know Stanley?" Said Mr. Grauso. Popeye raised his eyes humbly toward Mr. Grauso and jokingly stated, "You could've warned me..but instead you set me up." Both men laughed.

"What can I say?" said Mr. Grauso. "He's his father's son...he learned from the best!"

"I'll say he did. It's a good thing you came when you did. I was getting ready to throw my watch on the table." Stanley grabbed his things and bid his farewell to the boys. Mr.

Grauso, Popeye and Stanley left the warehouse and walked over to Mr. Grauso's new automobile. Stanley secretly nudged Popeye as Mr. Grauso walked a few steps ahead. Stanley hinted - with Popeye barely reading his lips- that Popeye inquire about Stanley coming back. Popeye spoke as if he'd almost forgotten.

"So Mr. Grauso...will Stanley be joining us again soon...We'd love to get a few of the other boys over...watch him clean them out. You know?" Mr. Grauso looked at Stanley. Stanley's expression obviously begging for Mr. Grauso's approval.

"Stanley and I'll both see you next week..." Stanley's eyes widened with excitement. Popeye tapped the top of the automobile as Mr. Grauso pulled off. Stanley remained quiet and a bit aloof yet happy for the remainder of the ride home. His quietness was a tactic used from past experience: once Mr. Grauso had given consent on an issue, visiting the matter again would sometimes cause his father to think about it and later retract his consent on the issue. Mr. Grauso pulled up to the house and blew the horn. Mrs. Grauso, Theresa, Rose and Freddy all came running outside excited about the family's new car. Before exiting the car, Mr. Grauso leaned over and whispered to Stanley, " I want you to get a lot of rest and focus Stanley. Next week you start work for Don Ernesto." Stanley smiled in amazement. He embraced his father as if he had been informed about being accepted into a top college of some sort.

"I won't let you down Papa," he said while letting go of his embrace. The two then joined the family for what was left of a peaceful Sunday evening.

CHAPTER SIX

"DON'T YOU EVER RAISE YOUR VOICE IN MY HOUSE AGAIN! YOU GOT THAT? I BROUGHT YOU INTO THIS WORLD AND BELIEVE ME...I'LL TAKE YOUR LITTLE FAT ASS OUT!" Mrs. Grauso could easily hear Mr. Grauso yelling clear across the house. It was hard to tell whether it was her nerves or the walls shaking from all of the commotion going on these days. Several years had passed. The year was 1927. By now, Stanley had already learned to drive, purchased his own car and begun to experience the growing pains associated with being an independent seventeen-year old drop out.

"SIT YOUR ASS DOWN...I'LL TELL YOU WHEN THIS DISCUSSION IS OVER!" Mrs. Grauso chuckled a bit as only a mother would. It was rare for Stanley and Mr. Grauso to be at odds. Usually, it was Mrs. Grauso doing the screaming with Mr. Grauso barely intervening. But now the tables had turned and Stanley's attitude had made its way over to the testing side of his father.

Mr. Grauso came storming into the kitchen. The front of his hair stood oddly out of place clearly disarrayed from all of the yelling and screaming. Mrs. Grauso tucked her chin in to avoid her soft laughter from being heard.

"That damn son of yours..." Mr. Grauso frustratingly stated.

"Oh, so now he's my son."

"I'm not in the mood Josephine..." Mr. Grauso walked over to the refrigerator and pulled himself out a cold beer. Mrs. Grauso walked over and gently stroked her husband's back.

"Alex, is it that bad?...Surely you must have known that times like these were bound to come...So now it's a big deal because he's not listening to you ..." Mr. Grauso took a swig of the ice cold beer in his hand then pressed the cold can onto his forehead alleviating some of the pressure caused by his pounding headache.

"What do you mean I should've seen this day coming? And now that he's not listening to me? What's that supposed to mean?"

"It's not like he's a little kid anymore, Alex. Stanley's almost a grown man. So it's obvious that the older he gets, he's going to want to do as he pleases." Alexander attempted to speak but Mrs. Grauso interrupted.

"You've always treated him as if he were an adult; even from a child. Now the older he gets, he's supposed to listen as any normal child would?" She placed her hand onto her husband's face and gently caressed it.

"It doesn't work that way, my love. Can't bend a tree when it's full grown... If you wanted him to be a respectful child, then you should have reared him up as a respectful child... like our other children, not some type of friend who happens to be your child."

For a brief moment, there was a small window of silence. Mr. Grauso leaned back against the kitchen counter. Deep down he knew that his wife was right and although his expression clearly stated it, his pride just wouldn't let the words come out of his mouth. Instead, he placed the half empty can of beer on the table and without saying a word, walked back into his office and continued his discussion with Stanley. Stanley was taken completely by surprise by the manner in which his father stormed into the room.

"After all these years Stanley...I gave you everything...and now you want to repay me by leaving. What are you going to tell Don Ernesto?" Stanley opened his mouth in an attempt to speak but before a single word could make its way out, he found himself being interrupted by Mr. Grauso again.

"And who are these hoods you want to run with anyway? Does this have anything to do with that clown, Phil Musica!"

"Its my friend Big Dietz...and we're not hoods...we're business men," Stanley said in a sarcastic tone.

"Dietz? You mean the kid who moved to New York to become a pimp? Don't give me that business men shit, Stanley! If all you're doing is running numbers and hanging around with pimps day in and day out...damn it, that makes you a hood."

78

"How is it so different from what we do, Papa?"

"What do you mean how is it any different? What are you, blind?!" Mr. Grauso walked over to Stanley.

"Think Stanley," he said while pointing his index finger repeatedly onto the side of Stanley's head.

"Where's the legitimacy in what you're doing?" Stanley just stared at his father not knowing what to make of his question.

"None of this is legitimate, Papa...I don't understand."

"Exactly! At least with my bail bondsman business and my job with the courts, people respect me as a legitimate, hardworking business man. Do you think that you can just move to New York city and parade around in the finest clothes, drive a nice car, stay in fancy hotels, spend money like its fucking water with vast amounts of time on your hands without anyone noticing? You're kidding yourself. "

"Papa, Big Dietz says things are different now..."

"Shut up and listen..."

"Where was I?...Oh yeah...and when people notice they talk and when people talk, word gets around and when word gets around that's when the boys in blue and their little flunkies start investigating you and sticking their hands in your pockets. Is that what you want...to work for the NYPD? Because believe me, no one's on the take like those sons of bitches!"

Stanley listened half hearted. The chances of Mr. Grauso's words being planted deep enough to convince him otherwise were slim to none.

"Dietz has been there for years, Papa...he ain't hurting. In fact, he says there's no trouble at all."

"That's what they all say..." It was evident that Mr. Grauso wasn't going to change Stanley's mind on the issue of leaving. However, he was still Stanley's father and played that card quite frequently.

"Look Stanley, you're about to turn eighteen...if you feel the same way a year from now, you're free to go." Stanley's facial expression hardened.

"Why can't I go...".

Mr. Grauso interrupted, "Two reasons, one:because I'm your father and like I said you're not quite eighteen, two: because what I say goes. You got that?" Stanley continued mumbling about the issue.

"Look Stanley, I ain't your mother. I won't hit you in the mouth with a wooden spoon..."

"...And what's that supposed to mean?" asked Stanley. Mr. Grauso walked over to his desk and took a seat. He slowly balled his fist, raised it toward Stanley then calmly spoke.

"I'll pop you in the chops with this...okay?" Stanley kept his eyes glued on Mr. Grauso's fist. Mr. Grauso's facial expression remained stern while Stanley paced back and forth with a three dollar smirk on his face. His stomach filled with butterflies and his heart raced at the mere thought of his father making good on his promise.

"One year...you promise?"Stanley spoke as if he were in charge of negotiations at a table of some sort.

"My word is my word, Stanley." Stanley stuck out his hand and remained quite forward with making eye contact with his father.

"Shake on it..." he said. Mr. Grauso took one look at Stanley's extended hand then intensely stared back at Stanley. After about fifteen seconds, Stanley nervously pulled his hand back and left his fathers office. Stanley moved as if he were taking small strides across a pond of ice in a desperate attempt not to fall.

Mr. Grauso could easily see that he had gotten the best of Stanley's inner tough guy. He thought to himself, "And this kid thinks he's ready to take on the world...give me a fucking break!"

****

Several weeks had passed since the blowout between Stanley and Mr. Grauso. Alexander had never expected to be as close to losing Stanley as he was. In his own mind, he had written the script of how Stanley's life would play out as long as he was in control. A building rift between family (especially Italian families) was past bearing and almost unheard of in those days. He had begun to see the negative qualities he had instilled in Stanley. Mrs. Grauso often reminded him of the example it would set for the younger siblings if Stanley were allowed to continue living under his roof with no accountability. Her point haunted Mr. Grauso to some degree. However, the pride and refusal of admitting where he had gone wrong with Stanley was always enough to wipe away the feelings of doubt deep within him.

Salvatore had taken the initiative to move to Chicago. It was official, he wanted nothing to do with the family. By family, he meant Mr. Grauso and Stanley. There was never any outward aggression displayed by Salvatore toward Stanley or Mr. Grauso but the many letters and phone calls addressed to Mrs. Grauso and the other siblings versus the few, if any, received by Stanley and Mr. Grauso made it quite obvious where Salvatore's priorities were. Salvatore never agreed with the manner in which Stanley was allowed to conduct his life nor did he agree with the favoritism displayed by Mr. Grauso toward Stanley. Moving to Chicago was just his way of lashing out for all of the years of not being the favored son.

★★★★★★★★★★★★★★★

"Three thousand-sixty, Three thousand-eighty...Thirty-one hundred." Stanley was all teeth and cheeks with a smile that appeared to be nailed open while counting his secret stash. Between booze runs, filling in on occasions at Don Ernesto's gambling spots and the normal routine runs for Mr. Grauso, Stanley fared pretty well financially. Morally however, one could easily see a serious decline in Stanley's character (not that he was some angel who fell from grace to begin with). Spiritual bankruptcy was eventually what Stanley was heading for if he himself did not recognize the error of his own volitions and change. His lifestyle along with the choices he had made caused him to live somewhat frantic and defensive. He always assumed that others always thought the worse concerning him or that maybe somehow they had heard something concerning one of his many punk displays of street antics.

"Who gives a shit," was the phrase that played over and over in his mind like a broken record. His stubborn will to match the stares of others was always his way of dealing with those who "judged him" per say. Gestures of violence, outbursts of anger and verbal threats protruded from Stanley's mouth like a bullet ejected from its chamber toward anyone daring to lock eyes with the young stallion.

Stanley sat on his bed collecting his thoughts while gathering the money into two small stacks. He took five twenty dollar bills from the stash and crammed them into his right pant pocket. He stood to his feet then pulled his slacks from the tight wedge gathered in his crotch. The room door opened unexpectedly. Mrs. Grauso slowly peeked her head in. Stanley plopped back down onto his bed in order to avoid the stash of money being seen.

"Gee mom, can't you knock?" Stanley's ass remained parked and frozen on the money. He slowly placed both hands on the bedside in a desperate attempt to avoid any money not covered by his rear end from being seen. His stiffened and contemptuous body language could easily be spotted by Mrs. Grauso.

"Is everything alright? I just wanted to speak with you for a moment. That's all..." It was apparent to her that Stanley was uncomfortable due to her unforeseen presence. She immediately thought to herself, "What's this kid hiding now?" Mrs. Grauso stepped into the room but remained close to the door. The tensity in Stanley's body language grew. Mrs. Grauso took a quick glare across the entire room including the floor. The corner of a dirty magazine lay partially in the open sticking out from under Stanley's bed. Mrs. Grauso blushed a little as Stanley's eyes traced the distance from which her eyes stared pinpointing the magazine. It was obvious they both were looking at the same thing.

"Poor kid's embarrassed," she thought to herself. Mrs. Grauso gently shrugged it off as if she'd seen nothing.

"I'll be downstairs. See me before you leave. Okay?"

"I will..." answered Stanley as his mother slowly exited his man cave.

Deep down, Stanley really didn't give a care in the world about his mother seeing the money or the dirty magazine. At seventeen he was his own man and would do as he pleased whenever he pleased, despite what she thought. However, a kid with a few odd and end jobs possessing three thousand dollars in cash, in that day, would be the equivalent to a child with a part time job possessing thirty or forty thousand dollars in cash today. That meant one hell of a third degree interrogation from Mrs. Grauso for Stanley and Mr. Grauso.

Stanley dreaded having to explain anything to his mother pertaining to his life. One would almost think his approach and thinking toward her to be a bit chauvinistic. In fact,

Stanley wasn't into explaining every detail of his finances to his father these days either. The truth is that Don Ernesto never really kept a sharp eye on Stanley at all, like he'd promised Alexander he would.

Stanley had taken on the alias of *Thomasino Bianca*, which was Italian for *Thomas White*. It only made sense since his father, Alexander, was known as *Charlie White* within the same circles.

No one knew Stanley's real name or birth identity except for Don Ernesto and Popeye. And since Popeye hadn't been around for months, no one could finger Stanley Grauso as *Thomas White,* except for Don Ernesto.

Popeye had gone off to Italy to visit his sick mother; or at least that was the excuse everyone gave to anyone inquiring about the muscular brick house. But on one or two occasions, Stanley had actually heard that Popeye had crossed Mr. Ernesto and wouldn't be visiting anyone anymore, if you get the drift.

One of Mr. Ernesto's bodyguards, nicknamed *Skinny,* would occasionally joke with a few of the boys whenever Mr. Ernesto wasn't around. Skinny would walk across a specific parcel of land, located on Mr. Ernesto's property: stop then tip his hat as if to pay respects.

"We miss you Popeye..." he'd jokingly whisper and while the others would laugh, Skinny would always reply, "I know...I threw the last spoonful of dirt in his face myself..." Stanley never inquired about Popeye or anyone else for that matter. He and his partner Phil Musica both were making Don Ernesto happy; not to mention a ton of money in booze runs and drops.

✳✳✳✳✳✳✳✳✳✳✳✳✳✳✳✳

Beep! Beep! Beep! ...Stanley looked out of his room window. Phil Musica was outside blowing, behind the wheel of Don Ernesto's Silver Ghost Rolls Royce.

"How in the hell did he pull this one off..." Stanley thought to himself referring to Phil driving Don Ernesto's Rolls. Stanley opened the window slightly and shouted, "Alright, alright! Give me a minute..." *Beep! Beep! Beep!* Phil Musica continued blowing the horn more recklessly. "Hurry the fuck up!" He jokingly blared.

It wasn't long before Mr. Grauso walked out onto his front porch. "HEY!" he shouted, "This is a respectful neighborhood. Go and take that shit elsewhere!" Phil Musica instantly stopped.

"No harm intended, Mr. White..." he said gesturing his hand as to imply that he didn't want any trouble. Alexander casually dropped his cigarette, mashing it with his size thirteen Florsheim shoe. Not once did he take his eyes off of Phil. Mr. Grauso only wished that it was Phil Musica's neck under his shoe instead. Alexander thought to himself while blowing the last drag of smoke from his lungs, "What does Ernie Cozza see in this clown..." At that moment, Stanley exited the front door onto the porch. Mr. Grauso muttered, "Get back in the house, I wanna talk to you." Stanley paused then whispered, "Papa, Phil is..." Mr. Grauso interrupted, "Get your ass in the house or the next time, I won't say it so nice." Stanley waived gesturing to Phil, "Give me a second," as he and Mr. Grauso walked back into the house. Mr. Grauso frustratingly pushed Stanley's arm down.

" Don't explain shit to him. He's nobody." After which, Alexander slammed the door, channeling his obvious frustration toward Phil Musica.

Mr. Grauso never liked Phil Musica from day one and on several occasions suggested that Don Ernesto get rid of Phil . He was much older than Stanley with the attitude of a biker and an immature republican. Phil had come on board around the same time as Stanley therefore it only made sense that Don Ernesto pair the two together. Despite Mr. Grauso's frustrations and dislikes toward Phil, Don Ernesto wasn't budging on the issue of keeping Phil or not. Phil was making Don Ernesto a ton of money in booze runs and gin mill sales and it was obvious that the money took precedent over any favors owed to or asked by Alexander.

Alexander and Stanley walked over into Alexander's office. "Why are you always rude to him Papa?" Mr. Grauso remained silent refusing to answer Stanley's question.

"You know what I think it is?...I think your jealous..." Alexander laughed.

"Jealous? He's a bum Stanley. Why would I be jealous of....that?

"I think you're jealous because he reminds you of you and me...you know, the way we use to hang out." Alexander walked over to the blind and opened it slightly.

"You want to know what my problem is Stanley? Look at him. I don't trust him."

"Papa, he's really a good guy. Even Don Ernesto thinks so."

"I know good guys. I'm around good guys most of the time with my day job. Don Ernesto wouldn't know good if it shitted on him." Stanley was surprised to hear his father speak of Don Ernesto in that manner. Alexander stared at Phil through the blinds, shaking his head questionably.

"When a guy that old tries to be that young, he's hiding something."

"Papa, all of the guys that work for Don Ernesto are older than me."

"Yeah, but they act their fucking age. Even the way he dresses: like he's ten. I don't trust him." Phil sat in the car bobbing his head while patting the steering wheel whistling.

"Come on Papa, I really gotta go. Phil and I are going to Canada for Don Ernesto." Alexander reached in a lower drawer of his desk and pulled out an object wrapped in a soft white terry cloth.

"Here take it..." Stanley took hold of the item unraveling it from the cloth. Polished to a shine like a black pearl was a small 28 caliber handgun fully loaded. Stanley's face lit up like a child's on Christmas day. His reflection mirrored its warped images into the handgun's steel like an image in a funny mirror at a carnival.

"Gee Papa, thanks..." Mr. Grauso patted Stanley on the shoulders as if he were the recipient of an honorary award of some sort.

"Put it away before your mother sees it." Stanley placed the gun between his right side and his belt then shifted it toward his backside. Mr. Grauso adjusted Stanley's blazer covering up the small handgun. "I don't trust that guy Stanley and I want you to protect yourself at all costs. I really wish you'd talked to me before taking this run all the way to Canada."

"It's only a few runs and then we're back to our New York and Jersey trips, Papa. Mr. Ernesto says that if Phil and I keep it up then he'll sell us our own trucks to go into business ourselves if we make good on the Canada trips." Mr. Grauso's facial expression stiffened and his tone suddenly became increasingly more tense. "What are you crazy? Your talking to Don Ernesto about leaving and going into business for yourself! And you think that he's going to give you the trucks to do it? Why don't you just say, 'Hey Don, I wanna cut your fucking throat! Can I borrow the knife?!'" Stanley wasn't up to his father's lecturing and began to easily make his way to the door.

"It's not like that at all Papa. I'll explain everything when I get back...I really got to go." Without hesitation, Stanley dashed out of the front door making his way to Don Ernesto's Silver Ghost Rolls. Phil Musica had began dosing off but suddenly woke up with Stanley tugging at the door. Phil unlocked the door.

"Damn kid, I thought I was gonna have to leave you." Upon Stanley making his way into the luxurious automobile, he noticed a smoke grey three piece suit, a powder blue dress shirt and neck tie thrown in the back seat. The clothes were balled up carelessly and had obviously been worn.

"Hey, what's with the suit in the back? Couldn't go home and change?" Phil Musica's jittery round about response clearly implied that he had forgotten all about the discarded garments laying in the back seat.

"Oh...those...I...had some business to attend to earlier." he said while pulling off. Stanley took another glance at the suit. His eyes then spotted an expensive pair of Italian cut dress shoes. In Stanley's mind the custom tailored made suit and shoes were somewhat out of a person like Phil's league. Although the two were making money, Phil Musica's trailer park demeanor and current style of dressing never dictated such fashion at that level.

"Those are some pretty exquisite threads you got there. Must be some pretty important wigs you were with..." Phil Musica continued driving and with a small breath of silence, avoided Stanley's inquiry concerning his clothes."

"Hey let's make a stop on Gilbert street. What do ya say to a little entertainment before we take this trip?" Stanley clammed up a bit. He hated going to the cat houses with Phil. Mr. Grauso's views concerning cat houses and prostitution rings were somewhat embedded in Stanley's obstinate mind but despite Stanley's allusiveness toward not going, Phil always found a way of getting Stanley to yield to some type of consensus in going. Most of the time, Stanley would wait outside while Phil was inside handling his business but on an occasion or two, Phil had actually convinced Stanley to go inside. The drill then was the usual: Phil would pay a couple of girls to entice Stanley while he wined and dined a few himself.

The boys pulled up to Gilbert street. Stanley thought it odd because the street seemed

90

like a mini ghost town. A couple of body guards were usually stationed outside for the girl's protection but were no where in sight. The headlights of another automobile sketched a slight gloom in the air as it raced by the Silver Ghost Rolls. The sleepy eyed driver swerved guiding the automobile away from hitting the Ghost still making eye contact with Stanley while speeding away.

"Did you see that?" Stanley asked. "That was Skinny driving..."

"Skinny's out of town with Don Ernesto. Can't be Skinny." Stanley reached behind him feeling to make sure his gun was in place.

"What's the matter kid? Your back bothering you?" Stanley moved his hand from off of his weapon.

"Something isn't right. That was Skinny driving like a bat out of hell and that piece of shit car wasn't his car." Phil Musica spoke to Stanley in a more adamant tone. "Look kid...I don't give a shit if it were Skinny's mother standing there with Skinny and his birth certificate...You ain't seen no Skinny!" Phil then opened the car door and proceeded to exit.

"Let's go have some fun kid." Any other time, Stanley would've opted to stay behind but this particular time the tone of the night didn't set quite right with him. Stanley hurried in behind Phil.

As Phil and Stanley both approached the three family boarding house's light green chipped exterior, Stanley noticed a bullet casing on the ground but said nothing. He and

Phil both walked up on the porch. Small drips of blood could easily be seen as if they were the drippings from an ink pen. Stanley stood close to Phil taking in his actions. Phil looked around the porch area and kicked a few bullet casings from off of the porch.

"Yep..." he said to himself quietly. Phil opened the front door and quickly stepped inside. Stanley did the same. Upon stepping inside, both saw an elderly man riddled with buckshots, several fingers shot off one hand, lying in a slowly widening pool of blood.

"Oh shit!" Stanley shouted.

"Keep quiet!" Stanley reached for the handgun given to him by his father. "What do you mean keep quiet! That's a dead man laying right there."

"On the contrary my boy, dead men." Stanley pointed his gun at Phil. Phil just laughed and reached over and snatched Stanley's gun out of his hand. He pointed toward the room off in a corner of the house. A small stream of blood could easily be seen traveling out of the room on the dingy wood floors. Phil Musica took caution, pointing Stanley's gun and eased himself toward the room containing the flowing blood. His findings weren't good at all.

"Come take a look at this." Stanley walked cautiously avoiding blood spill from getting onto his shoes. With their bodies hunched over plopped down on one another were two house pimps and the house madam: each possessing a single shot between their eyes. Phil Musica walked over and stood over their bodies then casually lit a cigarette. After an initial drag, he grabbed the dead madam by her blonde hair. Her eyes were widened and her mouth opened as to formulate her last words.

"Boy! Like she was staring death right in the face." Phil said with a sickening cynical laughter. Stanley darted out of the house dodging pools of blood spill and headed for the car. Phil laughed while screaming. "Come on! Your gonna see more than this if you hang around me. Can't be a pansy!" Phil Musica made his way out of the Gilbert street cat house. He kicked his shoes in the grass like a man wiping dog shit from his soles. Upon entering the car, Phil handed a trembling Stanley back his gun and drove away.

"Can't be no freaking pansy kid. Toughen up! Don Ernesto told me that he put you with me because you were tough."And not a word about this to nobody; not even your Pops or Mr. Ernesto. We weren't here! You got that!" Stanley nodded holding the small handgun in a limp grip. It was at this point that he knew that he was all in.

CHAPTER SEVEN

It was now May of 1932. Stanley and Phil Musica, both, along with Don Ernesto,

all continued to fare pretty well in the lavish world of bootlegging liquor. With the stress

placed on many Americans in those days, the comfort of alcohol seemed like the only

businesses to be in.

The "Great Depression" had officially set in burgeoning since October of 1929. The

stock markets were out of control and had crashed immensely with an all time low of

being down eighty-nine percent. Many Americans were out of work with unemployment

rates plummeting like an avalanche down a slippery slope and very few government-aide

programs designed to help those suffering temporary difficulty or those in tremendous

need were hardly in play.

Stanley and Phil could care less. It was "dog eat dog" and every man for himself in those days. Sometimes both men seemed to eye each other with a hint of mistrust every now and then. But if they couldn't trust each other, who could they trust? At least once a month, some type of trouble seemed to always cross their path. Anything and everything from frequent attempts made on their lives to being held at gun point and robbed of their precious cargo, all came into play more times than none. Stanley never said a word to anyone, not even his father, concerning he and Phil's many deadly escapades. Phil had convinced him not to utter a word to his father or Don Ernesto.

At twenty-three years old, Stanley was his own man, "so to speak" but relied heavily on Phil's judgement and criminal instinct in making his way through the life he had chosen for himself. Phil was as sly as a fox and to some degree seemed to have cast a spell or shadow of paranoia over Stanley. While Stanley reserved his own suspicions about Phil, a deeper mistrust for others kept him closer and more reliant upon his partner in crime.

"Believe me kid, your learning from the best," he'd always say to Stanley. Stanley would always laugh and retort, "I don't know about that, Mr. Musica...better than my dad and Mr. Ernesto?"

"Your old man and Don Ernesto couldn't smell me coming if I was a fart wit' a hint of stench in the air kid. Nope! Not by a long shot..."

Phil had convinced Don Ernesto to purchase a couple of milk trucks from a local milk and bread company going out of business. The trucks were in excellent condition and made great camouflages for importing and exporting the alcohol from city to city and across the border of Canada. From the looks of him, one would never know it. Phil had great relationships with affluent people in some of the strangest and highest places and had established several codes of recognition and respect along the routes and across the borders. Border patrolmen and officers were on the take and in fact knew which trucks to stop and search and which ones to ignore.

In addition to Don Ernesto's milk trucks, Phil Musica had secretly purchased two similar trucks on his own from the same company for the importing and exporting of hair tonics and milk of magnesia products for a small business he'd allegedly started. Sometimes Phil would cram both his products and Don Ernesto's products into one vehicle just to save on gas. Stanley thought nothing much of it at first but started to become a little uncomfortable upon noticing that Phil Musica's dealings increasingly grew within Don Ernesto's jurisdictions and amongst his people outside of the Connecticut boundaries. Conversations of additional shipments of booze outside of their normal routine runs, new faces or friends of Phil's showing up in Phil's trucks and extra wads of cash shoved into Stanley's hands by Phil started becoming the everyday norm. Stanley had three reasons of keeping quiet: more money, even more money and a lot more money.

The two were on their way back to Connecticut after making a stop in Jersey. Stanley rolled the window down a bit after Phil lit one up. He coughed then spat out of the window.

"Here you go kid!" Phil reached over holding the steering wheel in his left hand and shoved a partially folded and partially crumbled stack of cash into his shirt pocket. Stanley smiled while slowly pulling the money from his pocket.

"Go ahead, count it," said Phil.

"Whoa! A thousand bucks?"

"Keep doing whatcha' doing kid and there will be plenty more where that came from." A small window of silence passed as Stanley counted his bouquet of crumbled hundreds.

"You name it and I'll keep doing it," he added.

The two pulled into a rest stop.

"We got plenty of gas. Why are we stopping here," Stanley asked. Phil seemed to ignore Stanley while gazing into his rear view mirror. A car slowly pulled in behind the truck. Like an alley cat blinking in a dark alley the high beams of the 1931 Auburn convertible Cabriolet flashed on and off. Phil then turned off the engine of the truck. The car's engine however remained running.

Phil jumped out of the truck. Stanley gave his usual nod waiting for Phil to gesture as to wether or not he needed his help. "I got this one kid. Gimme'a second. Stanley waited as Phil journeyed to the rear of the truck. Stanley watched gazing through the side passenger's rearview. Although he couldn't make out the facial features of the man exiting

97

the car to talk with Phil, it was obvious by the man's attire that he was of a distinguished and upper class nature.

"Frank! How are you?" Said the man placing both hands on Phil's shoulders.

"Keep it down Marty." Phil whispered. "We got company."

The rear doors of the truck swung open and so did Stanley's ears. He clearly over heard the man Marty address Phil as Frank. Marty continued, "What the fuck is this with your clothes? You look like a hoodlum....a Bum!" While Marty laughed, Phil purposely ignored his gestures.

"Marty!" Phil blurted. Meet Thomas!" Marty shrugged a hello to Stanley as if to not give a shit. "Hey! He's Ernesto's kid so watch whatcha' say around'em okay?" The two men laughed while Stanley sat wondering, "Why would he tell him I'm Ernesto's kid?" Phil then leaned over and grabbed a small case of *Rx Tonic*. Meanwhile, Stanley kept his hand clutched on the small caliber handgun given to him by his father located in his right pocket. The two men continued joking and Phil seemed to loosen up a bit the further he walked away from the milk truck. Stanley could still however hear Marty question Phil from a distance.

"So explain to me the clothes and the milk truck again Frank..." Stanley reasoned within himself as to why this man would actually be addressing Phil as Frank. After all, it

98

wasn't uncommon to use aliases in the world of booze runs and crime. But it was the man Marty that struck an augmented but odd chord with Stanley. His presence and voice coupled together with the scenery brought a phantom and eerie like atmosphere to the scene.

"Energy's a bitch..." Stanley thought to himself..

Another truck slowly pulled into the rest stop as well. Chipped paint of a name that was barely readable and a picture of fish and chicken was the make up of the logo painted on the truck. The only thing readable was the word poultry and the abbreviations N.Y. A man exited the poultry truck and gestured toward Phil and Marty in search of directions. Phil placed the small tonic case in Marty's car as the man from the poultry truck approached.

"I need to get to the Bronx." As Marty lifted his hand pointing the young man in the right direction, the man softly spoke interrupting Marty, "I think I know the way Frank."

"What do you mean Frank, I ain't no Frank...." Before Marty could finish his statement the man pulled out a large revolver, pointed it at his chest and blew Marty about fifteen feet away from the car. Phil screamed, "SHIT! What are you doing!?" The man then slowly turned his gun toward Phil. "Get'em where I can see'em," he shouted. Slowly cocking the hammer back on the revolver, the man urged Phil to back away from the car.

"Too bad you had to be a witness," he said. "You got a family?...you know, a wife and kids?" Phil nodded, using every bit of strength left in him to breath let alone keeping his hands in the air.

"Well that's too bad old man!" The man chuckled while lighting a cigarette. "Maybe I can show up to your funeral. You know as an old high school friend or something. Bring your widow some cash. Is she good lookin'?" Phil's mouth hang open speechless grappling for words to say. *BOOM!* Happening all too quickly, Phil marveled while watching a small fraction of the right side of the man's head tear to shreds. The man's eyes burst open as if he'd seen his maker as blood gushed from the make shift fountain created in his skull. As the man slowly dropped, standing behind him was Stanley with smoke trickling from the barrel of his revolver like mist from an ice cold drink. Phil grabbing on to his heart seemed to have pissed his pants. Stanley didn't know wether to feel sorry for him or lose respect for him because of the manner in which he trembled tremendously. Marty's body lay at a distance like a rag doll while the poultry man's body lay lifeless sprawled out seeming to clutch the ground.

"We gotta go..." Stanley said quietly. Phil instantly grabbed the tonic case from Marty's car while he and Stan loaded there things back up in the truck and fled the scene.

CHAPTER EIGHT

Riding back to Connecticut seem to have become a chess game of the minds. Each man sat calculating his own thoughts, while attempting to calculate the other man's thoughts as well. Stanley's nerves were on edge. He and Phil had been in tight situations before but never anything on this magnitude. Blood was on his hands and guilt seemed to stain his conscience crimson red. A little boy wrestled inwardly with becoming a full fledged tough guy and Stanley Grauso had gotten what he's inadvertently asked for over the years. Phil finally broke the silence, "What you thinkin' about kid?" Stanley's bottom lip quivered speaking softly while unclogging the lump of air from his throat. "Of all things believe it or not? My second grade and sixth grade teachers..." Phil laughed cynically.

"You kill a man and almost get your fucking head blown off and all you can think about is a couple of broads behind a school desk who could give a rats ass about you in the middle of nowhere." Stanley's weakness became even more evident to Phil. Placing his hand on his leg he noticed that his pants were wet with piss. He certainly didn't remember that involuntary action. With his heart racing he remembered the one rule of eye contact and knew he had to use it but wasn't quite sure of where it would get him. He blared, "WHO THE HELL ARE YOU MAN? AND WHAT WAS THAT SHIT ALL ABOUT BACK THERE!" Phil drove approximately a half a mile with a complete window of silence.

"I SAID..."

"LOOK HERE....PUMP YA BREAKS KID! DO YOU KNOW WHO YA TALKING TO?" "DO YA?" Stanley's eyes widened like a deer caught in a pair of headlights. His emotions were at a point of getting the best of him but Stanley knew or felt this could really get ugly. For the first time he didn't feel so friendly or comfortable with his running buddy Phil. Immediately he drew his gun clinching it like a homeless man clinching his last meal. He placed his hand idle on his right thigh. Phil just laughed like the devil as if Stanley were holding a squirt gun.

"What'cha gonna do wit that kid?" Stanley remained quiet. Putting his words together carefully, he spoke, "Whatever it takes..." He repeated his words as if to convince his own self. Phil responded, "What!? You gonna walk home in the middle of nowhere? Put that lil' rabbit shooter away. Will Ya?" Stanley didn't flinch. "I tell you what kid....You shoot me and by the time you make it home, not only will the bottoms to those tight as shoes your wearing be erased, so will your whole fucking family!" "YOU OBVIOUSLY DON'T KNOW WHO YOUR DEALING WIT' S-T-A-N-L-E-Y!" Phil's blaring of Stanley's name sent chills down Stanley's spine. Phil continued, "Yeah! Stanley Grauso, Alexander Grauso, Josephine Grauso, Salvatore Grauso....You Want me to name those cute little sisters of yours too." Stanley paced his thinking, his index finger slightly scratching the barrel of the gun.

"My Dad will kill you!"

"Your dad won't do shit to me! Or should I say your dad can't do shit to me!"

"Well Don Ernesto..."

"Stop talking what you don't know kid. Don Ernesto is Don Ernesto...but me, that's another story altogether. And that my friend is bigger than who your penny pinching father or Don Ernesto could ever be." Stanley could taste lumps of throw-up in his throat making its way continuously to the rear of his tongue palette.

"NOW PUT THAT FUCKING PEA SHOOTER AWAY BEFORE I MAKE YOU EAT IT!" Phil extended his hand gesturing that Stanley hand it to him. "Come on kid. Let this be your last run tonight. Forget about what happened. Act like tonight never existed. Go home and pretend to have an epiphany or something....go straight from here on out." Stanley kept the gun placed on his lap while speaking both quietly and nervously. "I swear, if you don't tell me who the hell you are, I'll jump out this truck while its moving'" Phil laughed. "Go ahead, your better off and much safer jumping out of that door with me going a hundred miles an hour in this thing than knowing about me kid. Shit, if I were me I'd jump."

"So why don't ya?" Said Stanley.

"In too deep. Damned if you do, damned if you don't." Phil continued talking with Stanley as if Stanley weren't holding a gun at all. Stanley thought to himself, 'This guy is like some sort of Dr. Jeckyll and Mr. Hyde'. At times Stanley forgot he was even holding a gun.

"So how do you know my real name? And my dad and mom..." Asked Stanley.

"Well its like this kid..." And without hesitation Phil reached over blatantly snatching the gun from Stanley's hand.

"Gimme this shit!" Phil rolled his window down slightly and threw the gun clean onto the side of the road into some bushes. "Whatcha' do that for?" Stanley screamed.

"First things first kid; isn't that the gun you shot the guy back there with?"

"So what my dad gave me ..."

"Who gives a shit! Ya dad should've told you , YOU DON"T KEEP MURDER

WEAPONS AFTER YOU USE THEM!"

"Relax kid. Nothing's gonna happen to you. I like ya to much...Feel better?" Stanley crouched back in his seat folding his arms like a spoiled child.

"I'd feel better if I knew more about you F-R-A-N-K!" Phil chuckled while nodding. "So, you heard that back there huh?" He continued, "I'm trying to make life easier and safer for you kid..."

"You call it easy and safe now! AT THIS POINT!" Stanley asked. Phil looked over at Stanley. "You don't want to go deep sea diving kid. Ya ain't got enough oxygen in ya tank. Trust me, stay in the little three feet to ten feet swimming areas wit ya little bootlegging and running numbers but when you see the sign Shark in the water; STAY AWAY FROM THE FUCKING SHARKS!" Stanley poked out his chest. "What makes you think I can't swim with the big fishes? Huh! What makes you think I can't eat sharks?"

"What makes you think you can?" For a moment it seemed that Stanley was at a loss of words.

"I saved your ass didn't I?" Phil hesitated, smiled then thought for a moment. "You got a point kid."

"I could've easily let that guy take you out back there. He didn't see me and he certainly didn't see me coming!" Stanley boasted. Phil somewhat marveled at Stanley's

being puffed up about saving him. Truthfully Stanley himself had always wondered what

it was like to actually pull a trigger and while a part of him inwardly tried fighting off

what he'd done there was a monstrous pride building on the inside.

"So why didn't you? "

"We're partners aren't we?"

"Yeah...we are..." Phil nodded"

"So if you had to...let's say save my life again? Would ya?"

"In a heart beat!" Stanley said without hesitation." Phil thought for a second. "Well

...I'm in danger Stanley."

"We took care of that guy ...." Phil interrupted, "Look you sure you want to swim in

shark infested waters because what I'm about to tell you joins us at the hip. And what I

need you to do will only prove to me that you can swim kid." Stanley's blood craved to

know more and would do anything to be closer to this man despite not knowing his real

ins and outs. The killing scene back at the gas station had become like a drug in Stanley's

veins and Phil was the pusher man responsible for getting him truly hooked. Stanley

turned toward Phil.

"Well if they got a problem with you then they certainly have one with me." Phil knew that Stanley's adoration and loyalty toward him could eventually be used to his advantage. Pulling the old 'I'm in trouble' routine would definitely have its untimely and evil perks. He confided in him. "Look....as You probably heard, my name ain't Phil Musica. It's Frank Donald Coster. Some Years ago I bought a company called McKesson & Robbins. We sell pharmaceuticals, hair tonics...Shit like that! You name it, we sell it." Stanley interrupted, "What's a bottle of milk of magnesia and hair tonic got to do with trouble and big fishes Phil...I mean Frank."

"Quit cutting me off and listen!" Stanley's heart beat heavily. Even though he played it cool a part of him somehow feared immensely the man he'd become even the more drawn to.

"Where was I....?" "Oh yeah! You name it we're either selling it or going to sell it...." Frank gripped the steering wheel even more while the tones of his voice became even the more boastful.

"Now ask me why..." Stanley really began to think this man was crazy.

"Ask me why kid!" Stanley decided to play along.

"Okay why?" He continued rambling on, "I mean we got the booze runs, numbers...you name it! This is what pays Frank. Crime pays. I mean you ain't gotta sell no hair tonic Frank. I could loan you some money. I got thousands saved." Frank Coster sarcastically responded, "That's cute kid. Keep ya thousands. You'll need it before me cause you already don't understand."

"Understand what?" Stanley asked. "Two things," answered Frank. "One, the way of the world; two, petty crime don't pay...and this shit here ain't nothing but petty crime." Without hesitation Frank gestured that Stanley take a look at the crates of tonic and magnesia isolated in a certain area in the back of the milk truck. Stanley certainly didn't know wether to trust him or not but without hesitation moved to the rear of the truck. "There's a hammer and a crowbar on the floor. Use either to take the lid off of the tonic crate and the magnesia crate but don't open them all the way. Use the flashlight on the floor to look inside of em'."

Stanley inserted the flat side of the hammer between the two joining edges of the crate reached around for the flashlight and behold. Inside the crates were several different calibers of military machine guns. Stanley's eyes widened but not in dismay or shock but kind of like in the days when he and Salvatore would visit the corner store for candy. "Come back up here kid," spoke Frank in a commanding tone. "That my boy is the way of the world. Everything is an outward disguise for war and taking everything by force." Stanley knew then that he had gotten in over his head but his own fears mixed with curiosity fueled his metabolism like a high energy drink.

"So tell me more about this company of yours Frank. What's it called, McKesson and....?"

"Robbins...McKesson and Robins," Frank said convincingly.

"So you guys really don't sell tonic or any of this stuff?" "No, we do sell and supply everything and more. But that's on the surface. Those guns and grenades back there..."

"Grenades!" Stanley shouted. "That shit was suppose to be on a boat long over seas by morning till our little fiasco happened back there."

"To who, asked Stanley?"

"I don't ask questions. I just get paid and boy do I..." Stanley's motors began turning at the mention of getting paid more than he could even fathom. "So how can I get paid like you.....I want in. I wanna' know everything Frank." The truck seemed to shake from the flow of Stanley's adrenaline.

"You really want in kid."

"You name it! What's it going to take?" Without hesitation Frank Coster had baited young Stanley Grauso which made it easy for him to spew the next phrase out of his mouth.

"Kill for me....I Need you to kill two people for me." Stanley's only words then were

"When and where?"

CHAPTER NINE

Some time had passed. Stanley and Phil or should I say Frank Coster's relationship had taken quite the turn. Frank's approach had gotten a little more aggressive toward Stanley. Coming by unannounced and waking Stanley up wee hours of the morning well as the evening had started to become the everyday norm and although Mr. Grauso hated Phil Musica (or at least that's who he knew him as) there wasn't much that Mr. Grauso would lend his energy to in saying. Mr. Grauso had taken ill and was diagnosed with a rare liver disease in those days. His job with the court system had ran its coarse as well as his run with Don Ernesto. Mrs. Grauso opted on several occasions to take odd and end jobs cleaning houses to bring in a little extra money but Mr. Grauso's pride wouldn't let her open her mouth past the first sentence in suggesting such a thing. Stanley's hands had become full running numbers for his father and keeping up with Frank Coster's agenda.

Frank always dangled the idea of Stanley moving up the ladder in what he described as "the real underground circles" in front of Stanley. All it took was those infamous words, "You want to move up don't you kid?" And it was off to the races. Stanley would jump to the tune of what Frank wanted regardless of what Frank required of him.

"Loyalty kid! Nothing speaks louder than LOYALTY!" He'd always say. Stanley wanted to believe Frank and that's exactly what he did. It didn't matter if anything Frank said was substantiated or not. Frank saying it and validating it with a few yes and no remarks from a few of his flunkies, mixed with a couple of "okay boss" tag lines made it the gospel of the gangster world according to Frank in Stanley's eyes. True or not, it was definitely interesting the things Frank had shared with Stanley and allowed him to see. The two had gone to several black tie affairs. Attending were several "A" list people from athletes, actors, politicians and "selective business entrepreneurs". That was the term Frank had taught Stanley which simply meant that they were criminals who were great at covering up their shit. And Frank was a master mind at it.

"When people ask you what you do for a living kid, you simply say, Mr. Coster and I are involved in a few selective business ventures and if they ask what, you say sales and market share."

"What if they ask what kind of shares?" Asked Stanley. "Well if they get to nosey, ya' see: then you hold your drink in the air and act as if someone else is calling you from across the room. Then excuse yourself." Stanley had engaged with several important people of his day. Frank had even let Stanley in on several conversations with he and several constituents. Stanley was very surprised to hear how several important politicians were even involved in a four year plan that would raise enough money for Frank D. Coster to run as the Republican nominee candidate for the President of the United States of America. He had some powerful friends who at any cost wanted the world to be as Frank viewed the world. Innocent packaging and makeshift branding on the outside and everything forbidden and corrupt on the inside. Frank had often said to Stanley, "that's the way of the world", and that nothing in this world connected to a vast sea of money was ever what it seemed or appeared to be.

"Taxes kid! Taxes were the worst thing that could ever have happened to this country". He'd often explain or reason that if there were no taxes, there would be no corruption. Taxes should've only been for poor people and if they were the only ones taxed, they'd get off of their asses and make something happen. So because the quote unquote rich or wealthy had to be responsible for "taking care of the poor" (in his eyes), it somehow forced "good" people like him to use a more impractical approach to making money and Stanley took it all in like a sponge to water. Frank D. Coster owned Stanley's mind and everything Stanley's Father Mr. Grauso had explained to him when dealing with anyone in this corrupt and criminal world had gone completely out of the window. Stanley's runs for Don Ernesto even became few and far in between. His excuse was simply that he wanted to be in business for himself and left no explanation as to what he was doing or where he was going. Don Ernesto felt completely disrespected but between his love for Stanley's father Mr. Grauso and his newly found troubles with federal law forces, he had no energy or time to address Stanley. However, Don Ernesto was no chowderhead. He definitely put two and two together. Between Stanley's abrupt yet sporadic disappearance and Phil Musica's (Frank D. Coster's) makeshift resignation coupled together with vendors bailing out on him and getting there booze elsewhere, Don Ernesto knew somehow the two were responsible for his newly found troubles at hand.

One thing was for sure. Smuggling illegal firearms and booze that appeared to be the everyday norm of American hair products and pharmaceutical drugs was definitely more profitable for Stanley than Don Ernesto's milk truck booze runs. Stanley was all in even if it meant severing ties with Don Ernesto and a bounty on his head at some point. Frank D. Coster had assured Stanley not to worry about Mr. Ernesto and that there were ways and people around to handle him if it ever came to that point.

Although the whole Phil Musica/Frank D. Coster situation presented itself as a bit confusing, in a criminal world it wasn't. Stanley had learned all there was to know about this man and his alter egos and as far as he was concern both were real individuals glued to one soul. There were places only "Phil" could be caught alive in just like there were settings Phil couldn't carve his way into with a buzz saw. Frank D. Coster was the social economics genius. The criminal who had made himself acceptable to upper class societies,

113

what one would consider to be no more than mere white trash with an erased past and a get out of jail free card which allowed him to collect more than two hundred dollars when passing go.

His real name was, in fact, Phil Musica. A guy with a criminal record and make up a mile long. He had come from a family of crime. He and his four brothers were noted, in that day, for everything from extortion, racketeering and even murder. Although most of the charges, including several murder investigations, were unfounded everyone knew, from local and federal authorities to those involved in the criminal world lifestyle, the stamp and impression left on crime scenes by the Musica brothers. The sons of a New York importer of Italian foods, the Musica family had prospered earlier on in the import trade business primarily by bribing dock customs officials to falsify shipment weights. An investigation would lead to the Musica team being arrested in 1909. It was stated in the criminal rumor mill that the brothers all drew straws to see who would take the heat for the crime. Phil's straw came up the shortest. Philip paid a $5,000 fine and served five months in prison for the crime. The prison experience did not reform the criminal family, however, and similar behavior would soon lead to another arrest in 1913 on similar charges.

This time, a hair importing business started by the family after Philip Musica left prison had racked up $500,000 (Five Hundred Thousand Dollars and no cents) in bank debt based on virtually nonexistent security. A bank investigation revealed that the

114

supposedly valuable hair pieces being used for collateral were in fact only worthless ends and short pieces of hair. Federal authorities again sought out the family. The Musica brothers boarded a departing New Orleans ship in a poor attempt of escape and were later apprehended. Once again, Philip became the scapegoat for the family escapades and later would serve three years in prison. When he was released in 1916, the government cloned him as an undercover agent for the District Attorney's office named William Johnson. It was either that or more time in the federal pen. Phil, however, used the position to his advantage, making a lot of friends in the political and banking worlds. These people who became his everyday constituents looked the part of everyday working class Americans. However, with heavy access to ones backgrounds and personal records Phil or William Johnson at the time, owned backstage passes to some of the most prestigious peoples' lives. To him, they were worse than the modern everyday criminal because of their pretentious ways. In fact it was their theme of the American dream that would later gave Phil his idea of pretentious packaging for smuggling his firearms and booze. Look one way on the outside to cover what was really on the inside. One would ask why pharmaceuticals and hair supply? Prior to World War I Phil had acquired a poultry and fish business only to keep him close to the harbor with customs agents. His business interests would soon change after evading a 1920 murder conviction, from poultry to pharmaceuticals. He posed as president of Adelphi Pharmaceutical Manufacturing Company in Brooklyn. In spite of many "second chances," Musica appeared unable to avoid a life of crime; his new venture, a partnership with Joseph

Brandino, was actually a front for a bootlegging concern. When Adelphi failed, it was then

that Musica changed his name to Frank D. Coster. Hoping to put his criminal past behind

him, Coster managed to cleverly establish himself as a respectable businessman by

starting a hair tonic company that had a supposedly large customer list. With this

apparently firm collateral, Coster seemed a viable purchaser when he offered to purchase

McKesson & Robbins in 1926. In fact, for 13 years thereafter, Coster was able to keep

his identity a secret, he was even listed in Who's Who in America, where he was

described as a businessman as well as a "practicing physician" from 1912 to 1914. Coster

went on an acquisition spree at a time when the Great Depression weakened many

competitors. In 1928 and 1929 alone, he added wholesale drug companies in 42 cities to

McKesson & Robbins's American and Canadian operations. Five more firms were

acquired from 1930 to 1937. Meanwhile, 1929 sales had reached $140 million, and the

company earned $4.1 million in profits. You could imagine the hype and emotional rush

Stanley received every time he'd ask Phil to tell these stories. Phil or Frank, whoever he

was at the time didn't mind spewing out the energetic hype of his life's unfolding

revelations. He knew it was his way of keeping Stanley tied to the commitment of

loyalty made on the night there was an attempt on Phil's life.

The two sat outside one evening, in Phil's Silver Ghost Rolls after taking in a theater

show and dinner in New York City. Phil had actually purchased the car from Don

Ernesto months before making his ditch. It was a bit of a safe haven for him while driving down several streets in Connecticut and driving up and down the highways of the Tri - states. Many people still feared and respected Don Ernesto even though his empire had begun chipping away at the roots and Phil was into so much shit, the showing of his face had started to stink.

"I'm stuffed!", Stanley said while unbuttoning his pants and pulling out his shirt. He laughed. "What a life!"

"You like this life kid?"

"Who wouldn't?", Stanley said while gazing out at the New York Scenery. Phil laughed. "Where does all the time go? Look at that, 9:00 PM on the dot."

"You call that late?" Said Stanley. As Phil was parking the car after whipping it at a street corner he leaned over while rolling down his window. "I call that clock work. I call that on fucking time. That's what I call that!" Phil turned Stanley's attention to a man walking out of a fish and poultry market. Upon looking at the store's sign and logo, Stanley immediately remembered the faded yet still identifiable logo from the truck the night of the attempt on Phil's life. They were the same and thing's were starting to connect a bit.

"Joseph Cohen is his name..." Phil's tone changed drastically upon identifying the man to Stanley. His throat seemed to somewhat close itself off from its own air passage. His despise for this man was evident.

"That's the one your going to kill..." Stanley had no response or any words for what Phil had just said to him.

"Your not clamming up on me kid? Are you?" Stanley stuttered, "Not at all..." I just didn't know there were others to be dealt with that's all. "Just one more. Barnett Cohen is his name. They're brothers.....and they're getting in my way something terrible! So you with me or not kid. It's either that or no more gravy train for you. This is where your loyalty comes in at. Without hesitation Stanley interrupted, "Shit, then let me kill them both! I want to kill them both!" Phil laughed. "And you get all that satisfaction for yourself, no way!"

After placing a few cases into his vehicle Joseph Cohen got in and pulled out slowly, while driving off. Phil followed in pursuit. "Reach under that seat kid." Stanley reached under the seat pulling out a somewhat large handgun. "Now?" He said with amazement, "We're going to kill him now?" Phil responded sarcastically, "No we're gonna' do it next Christmas. What the fuck do you think kid?" Joseph's car was in route to Brooklyn. "So let me get this straight?" Said Stanley, "Why are we killing these guys?"

"Does it matter? Does it really fucking matter?"

"Well, no but ...." Phil interrupted "Look, these guys know who I am. They know that Frank Donald Coster is really Phil Musica. And if that gets out....it's really the end of the road."

"Why can't you just get one of your other friends to knock these guys off?"

"What don't you get kid? Frank D. Coster's friends know nothing about Phil Musica and Phil's friends better never come in contact with Frank's snobby ass associates! I got to do this! We got to do this!"

"So where's his brother?" Asked Stanley. "We'll get his ass in a couple of days trust me!" As the adrenaline rushed, the two followed Joseph off of an exit over into a secluded area. The man appeared tired exiting his car after spotting a phone booth.

"I'm going to blow this one's brains away," Phil uttered. But before he could reach for the gun Stanley leaped from the car and like a troll racing made his way over to Joseph who had traveled around to the passenger's side of his vehicle. Immediately Joseph became blinded by Stanley's rushing two hundred plus pound frame. Stanley's unfastened pants immediately became a problem as they started their journey downward from Stanley's waist. Stanley grabbed the waist of his pants with his left hand and pulled from his coat pocket the large handgun. That split second became enough time for Joseph to grab Stanley's arm with the gun connected. The two struggled in the doorway of Joseph's car but Stanley spotted laying on the car seat a small knife used for gutting fish.

Joseph had started opening one of the crates with it. After pinning Mr. Cohen catty corner in the doorway, Stanley leaned in enough to grab the knife and immediately caught Joseph Cohen under his heart with it. As Joseph paused with a ghastly look in his eyes, his grip loosened and Stanley snatched himself free, pointed the handgun to Mr. Cohen's head and fired. Joseph's body collapsed as if it were made of string. In seconds his spirit left and his legacy would be the lifeless remains of a struggle in which he didn't stand a chance. Stanley raced back to the car, tripping from his pants but making his way up. He and Phil Musica speed off with Phil screaming to the top of his lungs, "That was great kid! I didn't think you had it in ya'! But that was great!"

CHAPTER TEN

It wasn't but a few days later. Stanley and Phil were planning another hit, Joseph's brother, Barnett Cohen. Stanley checked the paper daily , his usual routine of combing the New York Times, but nothing concerning Joseph Cohen's murder or body had surfaced. A part of Stanley actually felt on edge or even slighted at some point not seeing his "work" in the paper. A part of him wanted the quote unquote personal fame. It only showed how sick he'd become.

He and Phil had stayed in a brownstone flat located somewhere in Brooklyn. Phil claimed that it belonged to a friend. As far as Stanley could see, the place clearly belonged to Phil. The decor matched Phil's taste in furniture. The ashtrays contained Phil's favorite Cuban cigars, barely smoked, just like Phil smoked them and sticking out of an overly piled high garbage can, was a can of Phil's favorite brand of shaving cream. Either it was Phil's place or his favorite hide out spot.

Both men were starving. Neither one at the time could cook worth a shit. Phil, however, had a five foot two inch beautiful blond food connection that worked at the diner up the street. She'd bring he and Stanley what ever they wanted to eat from time to time. Phil's food, however, would be eaten either reheated or cold due to the time he spent with the cute little bombshell between breaks. While Stanley stuffed his face, his meal wasn't the only thing he'd be enjoying. The cooing of breathless panting, bed rocking and mattress singing coupled with a few swear words thrown in the air every now and again echoed from the room in the back like a talk porn radio station. The panting was mostly from Phil.

"She's half his age" Stanley thought. "She's gonna' kill the old man!" After about five minutes, Phil exited the room and plopped himself down on the love seat opposite the couch Stanley was seated on. With his shirt opened and belly going in and out like a frog's chin, Phil reached into the pocket of his half buttoned trousers, counted five hundred dollars out in increments of crispy fifty dollar bills and tossed them over to Stanley.

"Thanks!"

"It ain't for you." Phil stated with cold egg yolk spewing from his mouth and pieces finding its way into his mustache. "Put it over there." He said, motioning his hand toward a three legged oak wall table that sat flat against the wall by the door. Stanley stood up and reluctantly walked the short stack of Grants over by the door and slapped

them on the table. The crispiness of the bills wouldn't allow them to stay closed so

Stanley slid the money partially under a lamp that sat on the table. He could hear sink

water running in the bathroom for minutes.

"Broad must be taking a bird bath," he thought to himself. Stanley's eyes shifted

quite frequently toward the bathroom while making his way back to his seat.

"Trying ta' steal a peak kid?" "Not even!" Stanley said with a slight chuckle. "I was

just thinking, bird bath for a bird brain."

"Are you jealous?" Said Phil. "Come on, tell me how you wish you were me with all

the cars, money and beautiful girls."

"Cars and money maybe but all of your girls, they cost you. Me, I want a girl who

wants me for me. Like my mom is with my dad."

"I got bad news for you kid. Your mom is costing your dad too just like my old lady

costs me. Either way, your paying for it."

"Hey, you watch what you say about my mother. My mom's a saint."

"No woman is a saint. Well in my book anyway. Doesn't mean they're not decent

but a saint, Nah!" Stanley seemed to become somewhat defensive. "My mother is a

saint!" Phil continued, "You're supposed to think that way about your mother, every kid is supposed to think that way but I bet your old man doesn't think that way. I'm sure he loves her and feels like she's a decent girl but a saint....." "What do you mean?" Stanley asked. "So you don't take it so personal, take my old lady for instance. Great mother, dresses nice, gets along with everyone, great education, you name it! But can be the biggest bitch behind closed doors you'd ever seen. Now on the outside she's politically correct but when it comes to my lifestyle, she pretends not to know but she knows just like I'm sure your mother knows everything there is to know about your old man. That don't make them a saint, it makes them an accomplice." Stanley's facial expression was of one that completely agreed with Phil. Phil leaned in to whisper to Stanley.

"Take this chick in the back for example. She's got a boyfriend, a wealthy father and mother, in school full time and comes here on a regular to screw my brains out for a fee. What kind of shit is that? But I bet mommy, daddy and the dumb ass boyfriend think she's at work being a good little girl." At that time the cute little blonde made her way slowly to the door. Phil's sudden silence and the manner in which he eased back in the sofa made it obvious that she was the topic of conversation. Or at least that's how she felt.

"I'll be going now..." she said in a somewhat embarrassing tone. Phil lit a cigarette, nodded and flung his hand in a macho manner. The girl looked down and spotted the money on the table partially under the lamp. Without looking back, she clutched the money in her fist quietly and walked out of the door.

124

"I think she heard what you said about her." Phil just shrugged his shoulders.

"Well then , she shouldn't be shocked that I'm the only one who thinks that she ain't a saint." He and Stanley both laughed.

"Enough of that kid. Today's part two of our plan. You ready?"

"Born ready, I keep telling ya."

"So Phil? You gonna' let me take out this bum too?"

"Too messy kid. Besides where's my satisfaction." "What do you mean, I'm messy?" Stanley argued.

"That guy almost got the jump on you...besides...." A long pause filled with tension seemed to come over Phil. "Barnett's mine!" He said as his nostrils flared. "Come on, lets get showered up kid and remember to do what I tell ya to do....and ONLY WHAT I TELL YA TO DO!"

The two men soon made their way downstairs into Phil's car. This time Stanley served as the driver. In fact, his attire looked more like that of chauffeur's attire rather than a colleague or a partner's attire. Stanley opened the door for Phil just as a chauffeur would as well. The two pulled up to a bar. Stanley exited the Silver Ghost, walked around to the rear passenger's door and opened it for Mr. Musica.

"Shall I wait here sir?" Phil Musica nodded. With briefcase in hand he entered the bar. Most of the chairs were still stacked on their respectable tables except for a few. A bartender stood behind the bar wiping the same spot as Phil stood in the doorway.

"What are you having sir?" He stated in a very polite tone. Phil politely walked over, pulled out a couple of crisp fifties left from his prior stack and threw them on the counter. The bartender anxiously reached for them. "Expecting company? What are we celebrating? What can I get you a round of?" Phil starred cracking a brief smile. As the bartender wiped out several glasses, he asked, "So what's the big occasion?" Phil reached into his pocket, pulled out a knife and lunging forward stabbed the bartender in his chest. The man's eyes widened. Gasping for air and in excruciating pain, his mouth motioned as if to make an attempt to speak but nothing came out save several drools of saliva. "The occasion?" Phil whispered, leaping over the bar. You can blame Bart for this one. It's you before me. NOW WHERE IS HE? WHERE IS HE?!" There was nothing to be said from the dying man, who's eyes remained opened as his spirit separated from his body. A cold ghostly chill came over Phil at that moment. He reached for the bartender's rag on the floor . He used the rag to pull the knife from the dying man's chest. Meanwhile, Stanley stood outside the car panting with a nervous twitch in his leg waiting for Phil. Phil wrapped the knife into the bartender's rag and placed the item into his briefcase. Phil headed toward an exit door located at the rear of the bar. Located on top of the bar were two adjacent apartment buildings. Phil made his way in as an old lady made her way out.

The building had an elevator and two adjoining stairwells. Phil chose the stairwell. Approaching the fifth floor, he stopped at apartment 501. A firm one, two, three knock instead of ringing the buzzer was the way or code in that day amongst crime family for each other to know or assume that it was someone personal on the other side. Dressed in overalls smeared in what appeared to be blood remains from butchered meat was a fair looking Jewish man who opened the door.

"Can I help you..." Without hesitation Phil pulled his pistol and shot Barnett Cohen in the face front and center. The young man fell backward instantaneously with a pool of blood running from an exit wound in the back of his head like a faucet. Phil raced from the scene leaving the door to Barnett's apartment open. The door closed slowly but still remained cracked partially using Barnett's rubber sole located on his left shoe as a door stopper. Phil made his way back down the stairwell, walking as if there was nothing to fear. Walking out of the building he immediately gestured Stanley. Stanley immediately opened the door.

"Everything alright sir?"

"Just fine. Just fine..." Phil spoke while getting into the rear of his Silver Ghost.

"So tell me all about it! What happened?" "What's there to talk about?" Said Phil. "Barnett is no more and I can go on with my life. I even got rid of his bodyguard." "Bodyguard?" Said Stanley, "You fought two men?"

"No they always kept the bar as an extra source of income but the guy or the bartender should I say was their bodyguard. He kept watch. Made sure no one went through the back to get Barnett or Joseph. Those guys weren't only into chicken. That's why they'll never find out who killed the both of them. To many people wanted them dead. Always sticking their big noses into other peoples affairs."

"So what next Phil! You said if I showed you loyalty, you said if I helped you with this you'd get me in BIG TIME!"

"Take it easy kid. You just don't go big time overnight like that. We gotta' lay low for a minute. Go on the lam. You know give it time to blow over. You go back to your old man's for about a month or two and I'll send for you."

"HELL NO!" Stanley blurted. I AIN'T GOING BACK THERE. ME.....LOOK LIKE A FAILURE! SHIT NO!"

"Kid take it easy..." Stanley pleaded like a women being left by her husband off to the marine core at a time of war. "You said me and you, we're joined at the hip! Now your telling me go back to what...." Stanley pulled over. "

What the fuck do you think you're doing? There's a fucking double or should I say triple murder within a two mile radius and I ain't trying ta be no where in site."

"Look, I got some friends here in the city. I'll hang out with them until you're ready

128

for me Phil."

"Kid, what part of murder don't you understand. It ain't good to be here period!"

"There's a freakin' murder everyday!" Stanley retorted. Stanley knew deep in his heart that this was the last he was going to see of Phil. What were the odds of Phil getting rid of him and he in return dropping dime on Phil. They both were guilty of murder so in essence it meant dropping dime on himself or running the risk. He felt used but what was there he could do about it. No matter how many times Phil assured him that he would be included in all of his future plans, Stanley knew that at that moment Phil Musica was being lade to rest and Frank D. Coster was free to move in circles he'd only dream about moving in. Phil tossed the briefcase into the front seat.

"Hey, there's something I got for you in there." Stanley cracked open the suitcase and in it was the knife used to murder the Cohen's bodyguard, the gun used to shoot Barnett and several bundles of cash.

"Gotta be at least ten grand or better in there. Just so happened that when I had to skin that bodyguard he had the safe opened. I thought of you kid." Stanley knew that the money had longed been placed there by Phil and that this was Phil's way of compensating him for his quote unquote, services. It was up to him to keep his code of ethics, slum moral, and take it. "Get rid of the knife and gun and don't forget to get rid of yours too. We'll head back to my place here in Brooklyn, toast up to our future and discuss our plans." Still everything sounded like a brush off but Stanley agreed and

played it cooled while he pulled off.

CHAPTER ELEVEN

Some time had passed. Three weeks to be exact and Stanley had heard nothing from Phil Musica. Both murder investigations had clearly gotten underway for the double slaying of the Cohen brothers that he and Phil were both responsible for. Reading the papers gave Stanley a little more insight on the actual connection between the brothers and Phil; more than Phil had actually shared with him or filled him in on. After reading several articles, Stanley couldn't help but feel like a duped Jack Ass. These guys were a threat to Phil and imposed no threat to Stanley at all. The investigation had clearly shown that one of the Cohen brothers, Joseph, had actually been subpoenaed by the courts to testify in the identity case against Phil Musica. Frank D. Coster had swindled many people, just as he'd swindled Stanley but this was for alleged millions of dollars. An investigation was clearly underway and now had come to a complete halt because the star witness had been put to sleep by the accused. So what did Barnett Cohen have to do with the whole matter. He was simply Joseph's brother and one of the many people Phil or

Frank had taken money connected to pyramid schemes as well as a legitimate paper trail

from. Others who had given money to Frank D. Coster clearly had gotten the message

after seeing or hearing about what had happened to their colleagues Joseph and Barnett

Cohen, making it even harder for the current investigation underway.

The papers even revealed that Phil had been taken in for questioning but was released

do to the lack of evidence and his wife's verifying his alibi that she and Phil or Frank be

were at his in-laws where she apparently was during that time. Stanley's mixed emotions

about being duped and used by Phil seemed to take an emotional toll on him. He'd always

either convince himself of some pipe dream excuse as to why Phil hadn't called yet.

However, he'd just shrug it off, refusing to let his seared conscious play even a little roll

in his life's road to redemption. The pathway of a slippery slope seemed justifiable and

quite the ticket for the frozen stiff inner man buried deep within and some how being left

with the murder weapon and a wad of cash didn't matter to him at all.

One thing was for sure and that was Stanley was running completely out of money as

well as a place to stay. In three weeks he had managed to go through eight-thousand

seven hundred dollars to be exact. The roll of big spender came easy to him. He was new

in the Manhattan area and needed to kill time while waiting on his savior Phil Musica to

come and rescue him and boy was he banking on it. He stayed in the best hotel suites, ate

at the finest restaurants, tried his hand at a few failing number and prostitution rinks as well as spent a load of cash on a revolving on and off friend who was a struggling actor by the name of George Raft. Between that and the home made excuses from his new inner circle from dying relatives to loved ones out of town needing operations, Stanley had turned into a softy being tapped out. Without Phil or his Dad, on his own no one would ever suspect this guy of hurting a fly. Like a dog without its master Stanley was clearly lost without his.

With a little over a thousand dollars left and a struggling actor for a friend Stanley had nothing.

"There's plenty where that came from!" Those were his words while playing the Big City circuit and by the time he'd began being tapped out, realizing that there was no Phil and no funds, his pride wouldn't let him real it in leaving the wind of misfortune blowing his way. His father had only heard from Stanley a couple of times during the three week period and even though Mr. Grauso's health had began to fail even the more, Stanley had begun making it a practice of avoiding time on the phone with his father due to their prior conversation. He'd always tell Mrs. Grauso to tell "Papa" hello for me, giving her the excuse that it was tough for him to speak, let alone see his father in such conditions. But the truth was actually that Mr. Grauso had approached Stanley over the phone concerning strong secrets surfacing within the rumor mill of the underworld circuits about the murders of Joseph and Barnett Cohen and how Stanley had basically been a pawn servant in the whole thing. More than the moral and concern for humanity, a sick Mr.

Grauso was more concerned with his son's contribution toward the "Family name" and how Stanley was perceived amongst his peers in the whole thing. Stanley had shrugged his old man off with the assurance that he was setting up shop in New York with an old two bit hustler pimp/friend by the name of Big Dietz and that he hadn't seen or heard from Phil Musica in months.

As for the world and everyone else; they could give a rats ass about Stanley, Phil and unfortunately even the Cohen brothers and others like them. Everyone had their own troubles and most of the world was climbing out of the muck and miry trenches caused by the Great Depression. The stench of suicide mixed with a demonized fatigue was could be sensed everywhere. The world had become a parched wilderness and its outskirts expanded like the plains of a jungle riddled with the blood thirst of animals. The second World War wasn't getting any better and it was every country and/or alliance for themselves. The Nazis were on the rise under the regime of Hitler and nothing seemed to be stopping their radical movement and anti-Jewish terroristic behavior and discard for humanity. Alcohol was on the verge of becoming legalized therefore business was not what it used to be. Don Ernesto had been arrested by Federal authorities with all of his assets being seized and both Stanley and Mr. Grauso spent most of their days shitting bricks nervous of how Mr. Ernesto's arrest would come back to haunt them both. With all of that, Stanley definitely thought it best in making New York his permanent abode. With a little over six-hundred dollars in his pockets, he packed up and headed to Albany

134

where he had heard that his longtime friend Big Dietz was staying. Dietz was the type who never kept a permanent working phone number but always made it his business to keep in contact with his closest friends only to give them an update if their was an address change. He had always told Stanley that the booze business would come to an end but the business of sex would never go under. Prostitution rings were his thing and setting up local houses with their positioning madams was his method of madness in running them.

"No male pimps!" He'd always say. "Give a broad a little power and you still can control them. Give that same power to a guy and somebody's gonna wind up getting hurt." So Stanley went to Albany in hopes of finding his friend. He never really anticipated needing Dietz for anything so Stanley never really wrote down or remembered the address Big Dietz had given him. All he remembered was Dietz telling him that it had gotten hot in the Bronx and he was going to Albany but after a day or two it didn't take Stanley long at all in finding his pimping comrade. All he had to do was ask around inquiring on where to get the best girl action and low and behold, the two find themselves in each others company.

Dietz began immediately showing Stanley what he called the true ropes to the business of "girlz". As usual, Stanley seemed to catch on quick; as was the case with anything crooked and scheming. Dietz had given Stanley some incentive if he'd learn really quick. "I'm gonna take you to meet the boss!" He'd always say. "But first you gotta make me look good, Stanley!" By making him look good, Big Dietz wanted Stanley to pretty much be able to run things on his own without having to be baby sat. Dietz's boss, Charlie Luciano was a well known trouble maker straight from Sicily. In addition to being well known he was rich and had everything in his pocket from politicians to cops and even murderers. Luciano had come over from Sicily, a town primarily known for its sulfur mines. He along with his partner, Meyer Lansky had an iron grip on crime in those days. His name was better than money and his association was more than any credit line you could apply for within those circles. Luciano and Lansky had made a name and a deeply revered reputation for themselves. Their approach to crime was simple. The more organized the harder it would become to brand as crime or criminal despite the many unfounded and unsubstantiated criminal activities connected to their inner and outer circles had become. Legal business during the day and hard crime outside of business hours was his motto. Dietz met with Luciano only on a few occasions; maybe to or three times a month the most. As time passed, Dietz wouldn't allow Stanley in the meetings at the 57th Street Coffee house. He often explained to Stanley that Luciano would let him know when it was cool to bring Stanley through but until then Stanley was urged to play the hand he was dealt and to be happy he wasn't in the street. At that time there was nothing Stanley could do but fall in line and be the best "Thomas White" he knew how to be. The two sat in Dietz's automobile one evening outside of one of Luciano's whore houses daydreaming and chewing the fat.

"This shit is for the birds man! I'm telling you..." Said Stanley. "What are you telling the boss about me Dietz? By now he should be begging you to meet me!" "On what pretense Thomas? So what! You ran a little booze, you got a lot of mouth, Charles White is your dad, Don Ernesto might put in a good word for you...and what good is that shit? Huh?! The Feds are about to really be all up his ass, his wife's ass and if he's got a dog, his dog's ass too. That shit will only get you somewhere in Connecticut, Thomas." Big Dietz slowly rolled down the automobile's window about half way, lit up a cigarette, took a long toke and gave smoke to the wind. He then turned to Stanley and said, "Look Thomas, these guys out here ain't like the boss's in Connecticut. Dietz looked straight ahead as if the car were moving and his eyes were fixed on a specific destination. "Shit man, they ain't like any of the boss's from anywhere. Their grip on this city is like no other I've seen. The only reason I'm in business with Luciano and Lansky today is for two reasons."

"And what two reasons would that be?" Asked Stanley.

"To remain alive and to be able to be in business!" Dietz responded.

"Come on these sons of bitches bleed like any one else! You scared?! Gimme' a break!" "STANLEY! Listen to me! Don't let your Connecticut tough boy attitude getchu' out here only to get your chunky ass blown to smithereens!" Dietz leaned back in the automobile's seat. Shaking his head as to pondering what he'd only had experienced with Mr. Luciano. "Sometimes I wonder if this ass hole could bleed like a regular human..." Then blurted, "I mean it Thomas, you can go back home with that attitude cause I ain't dying for you and no one else."

"What do ya' mean Dietz? Who's asking you to die?"

"When you don't play by the rules here Tommie, you die! It's that simple!"

"I don't get how wanting to move up the ladder constitutes you having to get killed. The shit just doesn't make any sense Dietz! I mean, if you don't want to introduce me to your guy then say so!" Dietz starred at Stanley. After taking the last drag of his cigarette he mashed the head of it against the car then flicked it off at a distance with his middle finger. He whispered, "Dammit' the damn thing's still lit." "You see that lil' bud. That's you all day Tommie!"

"How so?

"How so? You ask me how so? That little bud as long as its still lit has enough spark to cause one of the biggest forest fires. All it takes is a connection! It's supposed to be out but carelessness is all it takes and the whole world goes up in flames."

"So now I have the brains of careless cigarette bud? Is that it?"

"No, I must have to even be dealing with you. All you care about is making a connection to something you know nothing about. One wrong word, one wrong move and not only is it your ass but its my ass and my head for bringing you in. Everything here Tommie is about territory. You move in wanting to get ahead, these guys don't take to kind to that kinda' shit. I mean, I know you pretty well and kinda know how your personality is but truthfully speaking? You don't respect me!"

"Oh come on Dietz, I'd give my right arm for you and you know it! You do know that don't you?"

"I know you say that you'll give your right arm for me Tommie but your actions say different!"

"Really! Now I'm offended Dietz!" Dietz quickly responded, "Who gives a flying turtles ass Tommie! I should've been offended the minute you walked up in my establishment with your flashy clothes, playing Mr. Big Spender with my men and my girlz! And from day one your only concern is 'Take me to your leader!'" "Well I got news for you I am the leader. Respect that okay? Mr. Luciano put me in charge and if his men respect that then you gotta' respect it. If not then you can take your broke ass back to Connecticut and go back to whatever wasn't working for you so great out there! Cause if it was you wouldn't be here trying so freakin' hard!" Stanley could do nothing but sit back with his mouth closed completely at a loss for words.

"So those are my options?"

"That's right either fall in line or hit the road!" After a brief moment of silence the two burst into a short hysterical laughter.

"Just because I listen to you Dietz doesn't mean I'm scared of your oversized ass you know." Dietz continued in his laughter. "That's because I haven't kicked your ass yet Tommie."

"That will be the day when I die!"

"You bet your ass it most certainly will." At that moment a short stout unshaven man approached Dietz's automobile. His pants were partially undone and his steps were that of steps ordered by a drunken stupor.

"Hey, they say you're the boss!" He said with his words slurred. The man leaned over placing both of his hands on the car's half rolled window.

"I want my money back! These girlz are lame." Dietz immediately responded, "GET YOUR SHITTIE PAWS OFF OF MY WINDOW! NO REFUNDS! GET OUT OF HERE AND DON'T COME BACK!" Immediately following in pursuit of the man was an older lady screaming, "Dietz he pushed me and he beat one of the girlz up pretty bad!" Dietz immediately grabbed the man by the throat and punched him in the face. Stanley hopped out of the car, ran around to the driver's side and before Dietz could exit the automobile began stomping the man continuously.

"Hit a lady will ya?" He continued.

"Tommie that's enough! Tommie, that's enough!" Dietz attempted to exit the vehicle. However the weight from Stanley's chubby frame leaned in on the car door prevented him from doing so.

"Tommie, the guy ain't breathing!" The girlz from the house filled the porch area and began rooting Stanley on only making matters worse. Finally Dietz shoved the car door open forcing Stanley on top of the man. Bloody and beaten to a pulp the man barely groveled.

"Well at least we know he's breathing!" Said Stanley While the girlz found it funny and applauded Stanley, Dietz did not.. At that time a woman's voice could be heard approaching at a distance.

"Alright! What's going on out here? You guys trying to get me busted or what!?" Dietz looked at Stanley. "You've really done it this time..." He said while murmuring it under his breath. Slowly approaching the two was a bombshell of a brunette. Stanley couldn't tell if it were a wig because of the mere fact that he was too occupied or caught off guard by the moonlight cascading off of the silhouette of her hips coloring the shape of her half buttoned gown. His starring had become completely obvious.

"What'cha looking at kid. Put your tongue back in your mouth!" As the woman clinched the bosom of her gown she gazed intently at the man on the grown groveling and half beaten to death. "Who did this!" While the man groaned laying on the ground the woman bent down vicariously as to relate or sympathize with his pain. "What's the matter Mike? Too much too drink again? Hope this doesn't stop you from coming?!" She shouted. Big Dietz intervened speaking to the woman with a hint of fear in his voice. "Madam Corky..." He stuttered. "Ms. Flo..." I can explain. Madam Corky tending to the beaten man named Mike seemed to ignore Dietz temporarily. "How you gonna explain this one to your wife Mike? Maybe you should stay here a day or two...you know, till the swelling goes down. It'll be on me and I'll throw in a couple of girls for your troubles. What do ya' say Mike?" The badly beaten man identified as Mike, although badly beaten nodded in agreement to Madam Corky's offer.

"Help him up and get him to a room for a couple of days." She gestured to a few of the girls. Stanley and Dietz offered but Madam Corky stopped the both of them. "I said let the girlz do it! You two, I want to talk to the both of you anyway." Dietz gave Stanley a nudge insinuating his disapproval with the whole thing and how it went down. As madam Corky began to address Stanley and Dietz, one of the girlz began murmuring under her breath while helping Mike undertaking the stench of his alcoholic breath.

"Can't believe this shit! This guy hits me and now I gotta' help him out and take care of him. Business must really be bad. Now we have to add baby sitting to our list of duties..." Before the young lady could finish the tail end of her sentence, Madam Corky

142

yanked her by the hair, pulling her wig completely off. Madam Corky's claws sank

deeply into the woman's natural hair and the badly raveled wig. Corky twisted the lady's

neck causing her to do a complete three sixty facing her face to face. "Let me tell you

something heifer! If I tell you to eat shit you eat it! You got me!" The lady squirming in

pain barely answered Corky. Madam Corky rattled her head even more.

"I SAID DO YOU GOT ME YOU TRIFLING HEIFER!!!!!"

"Yes I understand...." Stanley hated the way Corky often treated the girlz. In his own

words, "How can one whore think herself to be better than another whore." But in

Madam Corky's world she was better than the other girlz and often made it known.

Corky let the woman go and began lashing out at Stanley and Dietz. "What are you ass

holes trying to do get me arrested and put out of business?" Dietz began fumbling with

his words leaving Stanley no choice but to speak out.

"You ain't going out of business by a long shot lady. You got more cops coming up in

here for snatch than you can shake a night stick at." Madam Corky stared at Stanley

with such indignation. "When I speak, its not for you to speak. You obviously don't

know who your talking to. Didn't your mother teach you how to address a lady?"

"Yeah, of coarse!" Stanley answered while sporting a sarcastic grin.

"So what's the problem!" Asked Madam Corky.

"When I see one I'll address one!" Stanley blurted. As Stanley continued going back and forth with Madam Corky, Dietz grabbed Stanley pulling him to the side and apologizing to madam Corky for Stanley's verbal assault.

"Tommie, you can't talk to Corky like that! She's the house Madam. I gotta let you go cause your gonna only screw things up for me here!" Stanley yanked himself from Dietz's grip.

"Get'cha hooks off of me!" Stanley fixed his clothes.

"You tell me one thing Dietz. How in the world are we supposed to be enforcers and protect the girlz and all but at the same time be soft and sweet as cotton candy. I don't get it! Gimme' a break will ya!" Madam Corky stood off at a distance while the two talked. Dietz appeared to be scolding Stanley but it was pretty hard to tell what the two were actually saying through the harsh mumbling and gritting of their teeth. Stanley continued, "The only person who's gonna mess it up for themselves is you Dietz."

"Yeah and how do you figure Tommie?"

"You see that bitch hasn't moved from that spot since we came over here and you know why?

"And why's that Mr. Expert?"

"Cause she's scared herself and don't know what to do! Who in there right mind will

144

let some Jack Ass that posses a threat to becoming some loose cannon stay. She don't

know what to do and if you show yourself to be just as week and scared as her then you

might as well be selling ass Dietz!" Stanley seemed to have Dietz's attention. "I've been

around enough cat houses to know that eventually if your too nice to these nut jobs then

eventually somebody's gonna get hurt bad or just plain old taken out. For Pete's sake

Dietz! Take your balls out of Corky's purse, fasten them back on and run this joint wit'

some steel! Will ya?"

"Look Tommie just apologize! Okay?" Dietz whispered. Stanley refused. "I ain't

apologizing to shit!" Stanley shook his head out of frustration to Dietz. And walked off

heading in the direction of Madam Corky.

"Where do you think your going Tommie?" Madam Corky lit another cigarette as

Stanley approached. Madam Corky addressed him immediately. "Listen kid, I don't

know what your motive is but I'm gonna see to it that you don't come around here

anymore. One talk with Mr. Luciano and he'll see to it that I get exactly what I ask for."

"I got no motive but to do what me and Dietz get paid to do around here and that's to

enforce the rules around here." Corky interrupted, "Yeah! You're supposed to enforce

the rules not make'em up as you go kid. There's only one boss around here and that's

Mr. Luciano and according to him, I make up the rules..."

"Listen lady I don't mean no disrespect but if lets say two or three guys right this second came here right now and pulled out their guns and wanted to take the whole place over, what would you do?"

"You threatening me kid..." Stanley laughed but quickly turned it off seeing that Corky wouldn't even crack so much as a smile. "Of coarse not lady."

"That's another thing. It's Madam Corky or should I say Madam Flo to you. Show some respect and cut the calling me lady shit!" Stanley continued. "Sure why not. As I was saying: if this place got bum rushed right now, what would you expect me and Dietz to do? Or would you think to just call Mr. Luciano while the mugs are killing up everybody in the joint." Madam Corky seemed to be listening at this point as Stanley gave his philosophy of underworld one on one. "Ya see...Mr. Luciano pays me and Dietz to enforce and if you keep being nice to the Johns that come through here then essentially you're letting them make up the rules around here. Now I've seen what happens when these stark raving Johns get to come and do whatever they want in these kinds of establishments. You essentially open up a door or a can of worms you can't close back."

"And what doors or worms might that be?" "That's when the crazies think they can come in and people lose their lives or get seriously hurt. All because the crazies get word that there's no protection over there..." Stanley stared off into the night sky, picked up a small gravel rock and threw it about a stones throw distance. "Believe me Ms. Flo, I've seen peoples' heads blown completely off because of fun and too much niceness. Plus you gotta think. How would Mr. Luciano feel knowing you cost him one of his most profitable houses playing nice guy." Madam Corky stared at Stanley for a moment. Her eyes seemed to have digested her lack of like toward him taking in somewhat of a care for his preventative measures. Stanley then rambled on a bit telling Flo about the murders he witnessed at the cat house in Connecticut. His gruesome account of what he'd seen sent chills up and down Flo's spine. He continued, "Plus wit' that hot shot lawyer boyfriend of yours, you never know who he's keeping out of jail or causing to go into the slammer. He's here a lot and you never know when his courtroom world's gonna cross paths with this world. You definitely gotta have somebody guarding these bodies Flo." Madam Corky smiled as Stanley's eyes traced each curve of her hip.

"Especially that body!" He added.

"So what do you suggest we I mean I do?"

"Simple, if someone's ass has got to be kicked you don't make it right by giving them room and board. You let him leave with his ass kicked and when everyone of his peers sees him they'll know that if they come here and misbehave then they got the same thing coming. That way the crazies stay in the cheap houses and the decent bums come here."

"I really like you Tommie....you got a good head on your shoulders." At that time Dietz felt it pretty safe to walk over to where the two stood holding their conversation.

"I'm gonna tell Mr. Luciano to make sure he keeps you on board. Believe me that will go a long way for you kid." Stanley smiled. Catching the tail end of Madam Flo's words, Dietz hesitated a bit. The look on his face didn't insist that he really wanted Stanley's name ringing in his boss's ears. At that moment a fine automobile pulled into the driveway making its way to the back. Corky's face lit up like a teenage girl with a high school crush. "Gotta go guys!" She said making her way over to the automobile greeting the gentleman with a kiss as he stepped out. Stanley joked, "She's his whore and she greets him like she's his wife with a hot cooked meal for hubby coming home after a hard days work." Dietz laughed after wiping the puss from his face.

"She's got something hot for him for sure alright!" The two continued joking but one thing wasn't a joking matter for sure and that was the young man's status and clientele. His name was Thomas Dewy; a hot shot attorney on the rise within the courts and within serious political circles not to mention the underworld scenes as well.

"That guys our ticket to the real prize," Stanley uttered under his breath. Dietz refuted, "watch it Tommie, stay in your lane!" Dietz grabbed Stanley wrinkling the shoulder of his jacket. "That's Thomas Dewey!" Stanley interrupted, "I know who he is shit head!" "How do you know Thomas Dewey?" Stanley replied, "There ain't too many wigs ya' don't know and see riding with Phil Musica." Stanley's eyes glared as if ignited by the wheels and thoughts continuously turning in his head. "Ya see, when I met him he was in the company of his wife with their pinkies and noses in the air at some function

148

raising money for Frank D. Coster." "Who's Frank Coster?" , Asked Dietz.

"Long story....long story." Stanley boasted, "I know more about him than you do Dietz. And I'm telling you, he's going to be our ticket to swimming with the big fishes." Stanley pondered his thoughts for a minute, "Now what was the name of his wife, she had a nick name for him. Phil and her....Oh! Frances was her name, used to call him....EASY FELLOW! THAT'S IT! They called him easy fellow. Don't know what it means but , I remember at this party; some republican shindig, she and Phil were privately teasing the prick and she places her hand on his chest and looks at me and says "I do declare (in her little Connecticut snobbish voice), anybody can get what they want out of my husband if they just say easy fellow." Stanley continued, "I swear, it was like some private joke or code for some secret society shit."

"Tommie do you know what your messing with?" "You obviously don't because if you did, you'd already would've messed with it."

Stanley knew that Thomas Dewey was on his way to somewhere fast and his signs of getting there by any means without getting blood on his shoes had shown little signs of ever abating. ThomasDewey was born and raised in Owosso, Michigan, where his father owned, edited, and published the local newspaper, the *Owosso Times*. He graduated from the University of Michigan in 1923, and from Columbia Law School in 1925. While at the University of Michigan, he joined Phi Mu Alpha Sinfonia, a national fraternity for

149

men of music, and was a member of the Men's Glee Club. He was an excellent singer with a deep, baritone voice, and in 1923 he finished in third place in the National Singing Contest. He briefly considered a career as a professional singer, but decided against it after a temporary throat ailment convinced him that such a career would be risky. He then decided to pursue a career as a lawyer. He also wrote for *The Michigan Daily*, the university's student newspaper. In 1928 Dewey married Frances Hutt. A native of Sherman, Texas, she had briefly been a stage actress; after their marriage she dropped her acting career.They had two sons, Thomas E. Dewey, Jr. and John Dewey.

Although Dewey served as a prosecutor and District Attorney in New York City for many years, his home or primary the primary place of dwelling for he, Frances and the boys was a large farm, called "Dapplemere", located near the town of Pawling some 65 miles north of New York City. Dewey loved Dapplemere, as he did, no other place. Some say that the beautiful farm served the purpose of Dewey resting with his family over the weekend while reminding him to "work like a horse" all week in New York City. Dewey Others were quoted as saying that the farm served as an over glorified dungeon to keep his wife and boys far away from his shady dealings in the real world. Dapplemere was part of a tight-knit rural community called "Quaker Hill," which was known as a haven for the prominent and well-to-do. Among Dewey's neighbors on Quaker Hill were the famous reporter and radio broadcaster Lowell Thomas, the Reverend Norman Vincent Peale, and the legendary CBS News journalist, Edward R. Murrow.

He first served as a federal prosecutor, then started a lucrative private practice on Wall Street; however, he left his practice for an appointment as special prosecutor to look into corruption in New York City, with the official title of Chief Assistant U.S. Attorney for the Southern District of New York. It was in this role that he first achieved headlines in the early 1930s, when he prosecuted bootlegger Waxey Gordon.

Dewey had used his excellent recall of details of crimes to trip up witnesses as a federal prosecutor; as a state prosecutor, he used telephone taps (which were perfectly legal at the time) to gather evidence, with the ultimate goal of bringing down entire criminal organizations. On that account, Dewey successfully lobbied for an overhaul in New York's criminal procedure law, which at that time required separate trials for each count of an indictment. He was known and quoted often as saying "ya' gotta know how to swim with sharks without getting wet or bit and that Thomas Dewey was doing. Stanley was looking for another Phil Musica to prove himself to and despite what Dietz thought about the whole thing, Stanley was determined in trying his hand at swimming without getting bit or wet.

CHAPTER TWELVE

Despite Dietz's advice of laying low and moving at a slower pace, Stanley never thought twice of conceding nor took into consideration Dietz's perception of riding the organized crime world's food chain. In some ways on one hand, Dietz was okay with Stanley's ambiguous tactics but on the other, Stanley's ways, although they made good with Dewey and Charlie Luciano, it had started creating a lot of tense relations between the everyday people in which they had to have everyday interactions with. So while the two were pulling in dough as well as minor rank within Mr. Luciano's circles, Dietz found himself having to fight every other day because of Stanley's mouth.

"Brains and muscles!" Is what Stanley would always say. Dietz would always brush it off jokingly by saying, "Yeah and thank goodness my brain's working because we'd be in a world of trouble if we ever have to rely on your muscles." Dietz had adapted Stanley's motto, "think in the direction of the money! Whereever there's money that's the right decision and that's who's side we're on!" Their practice had become showing loyalty but never actually being loyal if it wasn't benefitting their pockets. The two were on their way to meeting Mr. Luciano. It would actually be their first sit down face to face with the reputable street savvy business man. Charlie had sent for Dietz and Stanley, (whom he'd known to be Tommie) and the two had no idea as to why. Stanley and Dietz both had tentatively discussed what it could be the night before while counting out over thirty-two thousand dollars in cash across the bed of a sleazy hotel. Dietz repeatedly, although he loved the money, gestured of a fear of Mr. Luciano finding out about all of the side hustles he and Stanley were into. Stanley assured him, "If he thinks anything, the fact that we're going to show up should put his mind at ease." "What's that got to do with anything?" Dietz asked. "I mean it ain't like we have a choice! Do we?"

"Look, where I'm from; when the head cheese sent for you, he was the last to know and you were the first to know whether to show up or not. Got me?"

"No! That don't make a lick of sense..."

"In other words, they don't send for you to sit down and eat anymore when it's bad, Dietz. They send someone after you. Besides if Charlie wanted to get at us it would've been done already." "I don't get it Tommie. How you couldn't possibly fear this guy in the least bit."

"When he gives me a reason to be afraid of em', then I'll be plenty afraid of em'. As far as I'm concerned, everybody else he done hurt, let them be afraid. We ain't doing nothing but watching the market value on sex go up for him. Kinda' like his whore house bookies or something. You just stop sweatin' and looking nervous and things will go right?" As the two walked along the corner of 56th Street approaching a coffee house owned by Luciano on 58th, Dietz thought for a second.

"Tommie, you got your pistol on you?"

"Of coarse I got my pistol on me. I don't go anywhere without it. You know that!"

"I meant, I mean I forgot to tell you, we're supposed to leave our guns home when meeting with the boss. It could get real ugly if they pat you down and your wearing a piece. You gotta' ditch it, throw it somewhere." Dietz continued,

"I hear horror stories about cops on Mr. Luciano's payroll who show up wearing their weapons." As much as he didn't want to, Stanley reluctantly stopped at a news rack, purchased two *Wall Street Journal* newspapers and carefully wrapped his diminished thirty two revolver into both papers.

"What are you going to do with that? Why don't you just throw it in a gutter or something?" Dietz uttered nervously under his breath as several people walked by.

"I ain't throwing shit away! I paid good money for this piece. If your so scared then walk on the other side of the street away from me cause your drawing too much attention

154

to us witcha' mouth and your nervousness." Immediately Stanley dipped off into a side store, which happened to be a chicken and fish market. Dietz nervously waited outside. Stanley placed the carefully wrapped hand gun under his left arm and proceeded to glance at the fish located in several deep freezers through out the market.

"Need anything today... got some great lobster over here toward the back..." A store employee asked. Stanley kept his cool nodding as if to say he was fine and with a smile, he spoke, "Just looking, got a taste for something out of the sea, just don't know what it is yet." The store employee smiled in return.

"Let me know, okay..."

"Hey where's ya' rest room ?"

"Toward the back of the store..." The employee pointed Stanley in the direction of the rest room. Stanley heeded and headed toward the back. The stores rest room reeked of a strong combination of fish and piss. Stanley almost gagged at the stench. He put his hand through the flap of a trash basket positioned by the urinal .

"About half full..." He gently whispered speaking to himself. Stanley Gently placed the gun wrapped in newspaper into the trash can.

"Daddy will be back for you baby?" Slowly standing up, he could hear someone coming. He turned pretending to wash his hands. As a stout gentleman entered the rest

155

room, Stanley made a conscientious effort of looking down at the floor refusing to make eye contact. He exited the mens' room and made his way out of the store and onto the streets of New York.

"Come on man! What the hell do you think your doing? You don't keep Mr. Luciano waiting. Your really trying to get us hurt."

"You know Dietz, for someone who's kicked as much ass as you; you sure got a nervous problem. I had to get rid of my gun, right?"

"In a fucking meat market Tommie! Who does that shit today? Hide my gun in a fucking meat market!" The two sped up their pace approaching 57th.

"You know Tommie, speaking of my nerves. I didn't have this so called condition until I let you come around."

"Yeah! And you certainly didn't have the money problem you have now before you meat me either."

"That may be Tommie, but it ain't always about the money. You gotta' have some type of sanity in this shit."

"That's where your wrong my friend and that's where your nerves kick in at."

"I don't get it." "As long as you keep expecting sanity dealing with this shit, your delusional. That's like screwing a broad and always thinking, 'she won't get pregnant'. It ain't gonna happen no more than a piece of mind is gonna' happen for us Dietz. If you want a piece of mind then you might as well become a priest or something!" Dietz consented to Stanley's philosophy.

"I guess your right, Tommie....So how do you feel about meeting Mr. Luciano...I've only got to meet him or talk to him in passing myself but nothing like this." Dietz's tone changed as if he were a kid talking about an expected item on a Christmas list. "Never had an official invite to the spot with Charlie."

"That's something else you can thank me for, Dietz!"

"Yeah, yeah Tommie...so tell me how do you feel...ya' know meetin' the boss."

"As far as I'm concerned, its like meetin' anybody. To me he's got his weaknesses like any other man. Or should I say the same weakness as Mr. Dewey."

"I know whatcha' mean, Charlie sure likes them girlz Tommie."

"Girlz? Charlie likes the same girl, Dewey likes. I know! FOR A FACT!" Dietz appeared a bit dumbfounded. "Listen to me, you ain't heard this from me, but Corky's playing them both like a violin. Dewey treats her like she's his five star mistress put up in a palace or something and Luciano comes through during the grave yard shift on a regular when we're asleep or out and about and believe me, he's puttin' the salami to

Corky. I've heard it myself." Dietz laughed as Stanley rambled on. "And if you ask me, she likes it better when Charlie's giving it to her....That's why in my book, he's like the rest. A man can't be that strong if he allows himself to become that vulnerable behind a woman. Dewey's a lot more powerful than Corky and Luciano can't let him keep the bitch. You just remember that I told you, nothing good's gonna' come out of this." As Stanley continued, Dietz signaled him to stop speaking altogether. The two were approaching a coffee and Danish shop owned by Charlie Luciano. The place was often referred to as "the spot" and the shady dealings that went on in that place had began to stretch its arm across the new city of lights as well as the prominent state that held so many prospects for its citizens. Stanley and Big Dietz proceeded inside the coffee shop. A man stood outside the shop. His stature and persona appeared to project himself the size of a bronze statue. Stanley nodded in a nonchalant fashion and proceeded to walk pass the man. The man's arm dropped in front of Stanley and Dietz, blocking the two from proceeding any further. The two men's body weight didn't even budge the man's arm. "Not so fast!" He uttered pushing the two back a small ways.

"Announce yourself!" Before speaking a single word of rebuttal Stanley made eye contact with the man , thinking to himself, "What the freak is this guy made of? Must have a body shield or some type of body armor on under his coat." The man's eyes were stern and the more Stanley stared into them the more it seemed as if he were lost in them. His countenance seemed to be pierced and a small wind of fear for the first time in a long time drifted from his very soul. "Thomas White...and uh!" Stuttering as if he'd forgotten Dietz's name...."Uh...Thomas White And Big Dietz for Mr. Luciano." When the monstrous frame of a man turned his back to Stanley and Dietz, his shoulder blades spread like angel's wings balled up in a coat.

"What here..." He then pointed to a crack in the ground. "And don't step over my line unless your told." Stanley leaned over to Dietz, "Something ain't right about that guy. Almost as if he has no soul left. You know what I mean Dietz." Dietz kept his eyes on the man as he proceeded into the curtained off coffee shop while speaking to Stanley. "Yeah, wait until you meet Mr. Luciano. That guy's a choir boy compared to Mr. Luciano. And Mr. Luciano ain't even that big on the outside." "What do ya' mean on the outside?"

"You'll see soon enough..." Shortly thereafter the man came out and ushered Stanley and Dietz into the foyer of the shop. As the guys stepped in, the place was empty with a petite setting. No one patronized the place at the time, however over in the corner sitting at a table were four men conversing and laughing. While they guys couldn't make out what they were saying, one could easily tell that the manner of laughter was the result of a lot of dirty jokes and shit being talked. Stanley and Dietz were told to wait in the foyer after being patted down while the premature Giant made his way back outside.

Approximately a half an hour had passed and neither of the men in the coffee shop

159

had so much as even looked in the direction of Stanley and Dietz. "I'm getting sick of this shit", Stanley whispered to Dietz.

"I know, but we gotta' wait till we're called over. That's the rules and you ain't breaking that rule, Thomas."

"Which one of them is Mr. Luciano?" Asked Stanley. Dietz motioned with his eye brows while describing Mr. Luciano's features to Stanley.

"Ya mean the only one at the table without a jacket....wit' Thew suspenders..."

"Yeah, that's him...and please Thomas, no bright ideas." Stanley noticed in front of him a fresh pot of coffee brewing had finished.

"Can I get any of you guys some coffee..." Mr. Luciano stopped dead in the middle of his conversation. Two of the men talking with him glared over into Stanley's direction without saying a word. Mr. Luciano spoke after belting a soft but sarcastic gesture of laughter. If he smiled,his men smiled and if he gestured an ounce of anger, then they gestured two ounces. "What? This kid got no fucking manners?" You could hear Dietz swallow as the small window of silence passed. No one answered Mr. Luciano.

"I said, you got no fucking manners...this kid?" Stanley replied, "Of course I got manners. That's why I offered you more, I saw that you were out or had finished your first cup....and No one should let the boss be without coffee...right?" Mr. Luciano smiled

160

while his trusty puppets smiled in return. "Yeah, I'll let you get me another cup of coffee but I ain't gonna' tell you how I like it or how to make it see? After all, you should know how the boss like's his coffee. Right?" Dietz whispered, "You've done it now..."

"But....if You don't get it right..." Shouted Mr. Luciano, I'm going to have my boys here kick your ass for not knowing what the boss wants. How about that?" Without hesitation Stanley grabbed the nearest coffee pot, poured the coffee and spoke while grabbing a sugar cube with a small pair of tongs. "Black, one teaspoon of sugar stirred. Make sure you scrape the bottom and then place one sugar cube in without stirring." As he slowly walked over toward the men, Mr. Luciano smiled. "This kid's good!" In amazement he asked, "How did you know that kid?" Stanley handed him then cup of coffee. Mr. Luciano took a sip.

"Not bad... pull up a chair. You and your friend just earned a spare your ass pass." Dietz made his way over and as the two pulled up a chair Mr. Luciano interrupted. "No, better yet who gives a shit if you make great coffee. Don't pull up a chair. You ain't officially family yet. You do what I need you to do then maybe next time you can have the honors of pulling up a chair." Mr. Luciano slapped on of the guys on the back in a joking manner, "Gotta keep the help at bay these days, know what I mean?" All the men laughed, including Dietz. Stanley however didn't like being referred to as help as opposed to being called family but what could he do. Instead, he shrugged it off sporting a grin as phony as a three dollar bill. "I'm going to get to the point." Mr. Luciano said. I like...no in fact I love the profits I've been seeing from the Albany house. "Thanks boss!" Dietz

said. "I was getting ready to close the fucking thing and chuck the broads...but since

putting you guys on it I like what I'm seeing." "Well I can't take all the credit, my friend

Thomas here has played a big part in turning things around."

"Dietz, shut up I'm talking!" I gotta go, so I'm gonna' get to the point. I got other

venues...BIG VENUES, I'm doing but I want to keep the cat house monies going. I need

you guys to take over five houses for me. You do that and your in. You make me look

bad and your dead. Got me." Stanley nodded. "Just say where and I'll get it done."

Luciano handed Stanley a piece of paper. "Here are the addresses. Use my name if you

have any trouble." Dietz appeared a bit jealous seeing Luciano hand Stanley the paper

instead of him. Stanley took the paper. "Two weeks boss...and then can we sit down?"

Luciano replied, "I like this kid..." Stanley and Dietz exited the shop and without

hesitation were on their way to take over the five houses instructed by Mr. Luciano.

CHAPTER THIRTEEN

"**O**ne down and four more houses to go, Dietz."

"Don't go patting yourself on the back so quick Tommie, Mr. Luciano said the Bronx house wouldn't be easy to get."

"Who said anything about it being hard. All I said was, one down and four more to go!" Both Stanley and Dietz seemed to speak with an obvious frustration between the two. While Stanley's responses were more on the defensive end, Dietz's retorts and comments as of late seemed to come from a place of jealousy and resentment. A week had gone by since the two had met with Charles Luciano and the two were scheduled to meet with him a week later to report any progress made. "Let me ask you a question Dietz. I mean, we've been friends for a long time so we should be able to ask each other anything...right?"

"Where is this going Tommie? Please don't start with the aggravating emotional shit. Will ya?" Stanley interrupted raising his voice a tad bit over Dietz's voice.

"Can I or can I not ask you a question and get a straight answer. Yes or No..." Dietz

paused for a moment. "What the heck! You're not going to let me rest if I don't. Go

ahead Tommie, fire away. Stanley took a deep breath . Sitting on side of his bed in their

hotel room at first glance his side reflection in the mirror to his right instantly reminded

him of his father and then at second glance reminded him of his brother Salvatore whom

he hadn't seen in years. It had been months since he'd checked in at the home front on

how things were. Deep down Stanley was afraid of weaving himself back into the fibers

of the Connecticut scene due to the open hearsay rumors of all of the mess he'd gotten

into. Even if it meant being somewhat of a ghost to his family, his motto of being out of

dodge and being on the lam was his way of dispelling street talk coupled together with

rumors. After all Don Ernesto, one of the most powerful crime figures in Connecticut

whom Stanley and his father had come up under was in prison rumored to have been

going crazy. The villa was no more and all of Mr. Ernesto's prize possessions and money

had become the property of the state. A stimulus package one might say during those

hard times. How the mighty had fallen. Phil Musica even, at that time had become the

suspect of several federal investigations. Some of which included murder, conspiracy to

commit murder, charges that stemmed from his blood brothers' activity in the streets. In

addition major racketeering charges were piling up against his pharmaceutical company

McKesick and Robbins due to many investors not receiving their fair share of the

company's quarterly stakes from the company

. The thought of going back to Connecticut always made Stanley feel claustrophobic in some type of way. It was the place where his ghosts and demons seem to always come to life no matter how much or how deep he'd try to burring them. Seconds had passed but they felt like hours within the short amount of time he'd spent thinking about thefallen and the soon to be fallen underworld gladiators of his day. "Man I miss my old man and my brother for some reason.

"Oh boy...now I know its about to get thick..."

"What are you talking about?" "Whenever you want to ask me a question or talk...and you get to thinking about your old man and your mother...it gets real sentimental Tommie. And you rarely mention your brother...you've probably mentioned him once since the whole time we've been together. So I know your getting ready to hit me with some bullshit Tommie!" Stanley sarcastically laughed .

"Call it what you like but I just want to know Dietz, what's your problem wit' me as of late?"

"Problem? I got no problem wit you...Where is this all coming from Tommie?"

"My ass you ain't got no problem wit' me! You and I both know you ain't been yourself since we left Charlie Luciano's that day." Dietz proceeded to interrupt but Stanley was firm in his frame of thought and spoke over Dietz until Dietz was tired of interrupting. "Look Dietz, you and I don't ever need to be at odds. I'd much rather it be the end of us before we do something stupid and IT REALLY BE THE END OF US!" Know what I mean? I ain't got to tell you, it's a freakin' jungle out here....And if the elephant ain't watchin' out for the monkey's ass then....you got a monkey running around assed out. And I ain't ready to be assed out behind no B.S. I call it like I see it." Dietz laughed at Stanley's analogy.

"So you're saying that I ain't covering your ass..."

"I'm saying its getting a little nippy and I ain't feeling so protected by the elephant."

"You want to know what my problem is Tommie? I'll tell you what my real problem is!"

"Spit it out!"

"Ever since you came here and hooked up with me you got no respect for me. One thing you got right for sure and that's looking out for one ass and one ass only and that's your own." Stanley interrupted. "Now I'm insulted. How dare you call me selfish and disrespectful. If it weren't for me we wouldn't even be where we are right now. We wouldn't even be sittin' down with the boss. Moving up! Making this money....you call that selfish and disrespectful!?"

"SHUT UP ALREADY TOMMIE!!! For once shut up already before I take my size

166

fourteen elephant foot and stick it up your bare monkey ass." Dietz raised up off of his bed and for once Stanley headed or entertained what his friend had to say.

"What makes you think where you've gotten us is so much better than where I was trying to keep us? Answer me that Tommie!" With a window of silence closing Stanley slightly tilted his eyes in the direction of Dietz's feet.

"You sure those are fourteens and not fifteen and a halves?" Stanley laughed. However Dietz's cheek muscles never flinched.

"Not laughing Tommie...at all! You just don't get it? Do ya'?"

"I don't get what you get Dietz. Maybe I don't but to me this is better."

"And how's that! We just became two of the biggest pawns this side of the George Washington Bridge. You got us risking our lives for a man that wouldn't even let us sit down and call us family. I know Mr. Luciano. Guy's got piss for blood and ice for veins. I stayed away or kept my distance for a reason. When you came to me, you were broke as a joke with ya' big dreams and your expensive suits and your ring around the collar." Dietz continued, "I helped you out. Got you back on your feet. Gave you a job and what do I get in return? I've had more fights behind your dumb shit than I've had in my entire life. And do I complain? No! Cause at least we were still within quarters where I felt safe or comfortable. But this shit Tommie!? And you got the nerve now....cause we made a little money and sat down with probably one of the most evil human beings to strut your shit around town and act as if I work for you. KISS MY ASS!!!!

"Now wait a minute Dietz! Is this what this is all about?! You feeling like you working for me all of a sudden? What kinda' shit is that?"

"You just don't get it do you Tommie? I said you're the one walking around here with the attitude as if I work for you..."

"So now you're accusing me of taking over or something like that!" "You ain't taking over shit. However, yeah! I do feel as if you're trying to muscle yourself around to look like the new big shot in town. And what you don't get is that ain't gonna' get us nothing but in a lot of fights."

"Come on Dietz, Luciano made me and you...not me only but me and you enforcers. Don't that say something as to where we could go with this guy?!"

"Tommie, Luciano don't give a flying fart about you or me. Don't forget, I know this guy better than you do and if you don't see me trying to move up his so-called industrial ladder, then why are you? Doesn't it ever cross your mind that people roll a certain way for certain reasons?"

"Then why say yes to the man Dietz! Tell me that, Why say yes to the man?"

"You Jack Ass! Because you don't say no to Mr. Luciano. That's why?" As the two men finished getting dressed, Dietz's countenance seemed to change drifting more away from Stanley or caring about the current conversation at hand.

"Earth to Big Dietz....."

"You just don't get it do you Tommie! Well let me spell it out for you. THIS IS THE KINDA' SHIT WHERE PEOPLE DIE! And I ain't talking bout' people from the other side either. I'm talking about people like me and you."

"C'mon Dietz! We ain't gonna die....We Got Charlie Luciano backing us." "Do we really? Think about it Tommie, If he's so much behind us....then where's the additional men? Where's backup? You think we just gonna' show up at five cat houses and take them over on our word alone. As far as I'm concerned, this is a set up!"

"Set up!? Set up how?"

"Ya' damn right it's a set up. As far as I'm concerned that bitch Corky's got her fingerprints all over this one.

"What do ya' mean Corky! That makes no sense at all Dietz!"

"It makes perfect sense! Will you just shut the hell up for a minute and listen...." Dietz's anger became even the more obvious, pounding his big fist on the desk in the hotel room and frustratingly running his fingers through his hair while pulling out a few strands. It wasn't long before Stanley found himself pinned against the hotel room's wall

169

with Dietz's fist balled up against his chest and a hand full of his expensive shirt crumbled in Dietz's fist. "You get this through your head Tommie! I ain't ready to die or take one for you, Luciano , that bitch Corky or anybody for that matter. Stanley instantly conceded to Dietz's strong arm tactics.

"Okay, okay...either your falling off the deep end or your obviously seeing something I'm not. Now let the shirt go, take a deep breath....and while I'm ironing out the fresh wrinkles you just put in my new shirt, you explain to me the whole thing about Corky, dying ....the whole shit." Dietz did exactly as Stanley had requested. Stanley slowly sat on the bed and spoke softly, "I'm listening...You have my full and undivided attention." He said in a nonchalant but joking manner. Dietz, after composing himself began to lay it all out for Stanley.

"I know to you that this all as some type of promotion some way of getting ahead but it's not. I don't know how things are ran where your from but here with Luciano, I know how he works. If Luciano wants something for himself, I've never seen him just tell two guys go and take care of this or that without giving them the man or weapons power they needed. I mean come on think about it this guy's got governors, mayors, police officers and every kinda' criminal and scum you could imagine on his payroll and his shit list. And every body's dancing to his tune to stay on or get off depending on which list your on.....Everybody except one person that is."

170

"What do you mean except one. Who ain't dancing to this guys tune?" Without hesitation and a small manner of abrupt confidence, Dietz spoke, "Dewey...that's who." "Okay first you had me and now you're saying Dewey but first Corky...."

"Listen..." Dietz interrupted. "You and I both know Corky's doing them both. Dewey and Luciano. Now Luciano don't give a you know what when it comes to that bitch but Dewey we both know thinks that this bitch is house wife, house with the dog and picket fence material. Now if you and me stick around long enough maybe she has fears of that getting out so what does she do? She gets Luciano to get us away from the main house until he can figure out what to do with us."

"Okay Dietz, even if what you were saying added up, why would it matter to Dewey or Luciano that they were both doing the same chick. I mean after all she's a prostitute and the chief one at that. Ain't that what prostitutes and madams do."

"He loves the bitch Tommie. Dewey actually loves her. Never underestimate the power of a woman. You ain't never been in love so for you it may be hard to relate. I never told you this but on several occasions I myself have heard Dewey talk to Luciano like Charlie was the bitch himself." Stanley found that impossible to believe.

"C'mon Dietz now you ain't tell me that you've been dipping in the dope and booze." He said while laughing aloud.

"I'm dead serious."

"What did he say to him? I gotta' hear this and how come you never mentioned this to me." "To answer the latter part of your question is because you got to big of a mouth and a five year old bed wetter could hold his piss a lot better than you could hold a secret. Second, it was during the few times you had to run over to the Bronx and check on the numbers joint for your father. Luciano comes in right and I'm in one of the rooms with one of the girls relieving some stress ya' see. Anyway, Luciano apparently gets into it with Dewey in a slick way as to why he's hanging out at the Albany house at a specific time. Thought he had a trial or something. I know that Luciano wanted to see Corky but this particular time he kept it very reserved and you can tell   Anyway, Dewey told him don't question him on his whereabouts and to never forget who's in charge." Stanley motioned himself over to a small closet containing an iron and ironing board. Dietz by this time had his undivided attention. He continued.

"So they get to talking about Luciano bringing in these narcotics over from Italy ya' see. He kept calling the shit dope. Talking about how he was gonna' control the world with this shit, not to mention, make a shit load of money with it. So Dewey was telling him how he didn't care about the money and Luciano wasn't going to do shit. He said that it would make matters complicated for him." Stanley paused for a second,

"How can more money be a problem..."

172

"Here's where it gets interesting..." Said Dietz. "Dewey said that too much crime would definitely be out of the question despite the money because if things got out of hand people wouldn't think of voting a new prosecutor in office!"

"Dewey's running for state's prosecutor?" "Yeah! And that's why Corky's doing them both because she knows if Dewey wins this one, he'll definitely keep the heat off of her and if Luciano wins out well then her ass is protected either way." Stanley seemed to soak in what Dietz was saying.

"Okay so you got me Dietz but reel me in on how this spells trouble for me and you." "If we start stirring up trouble around town then the law ain't gonna' look the other way or think its some strange coincidence that all of a sudden trouble's brewing up around town with all of the main cat houses. That way, Dewey will be forced to back off from hanging around the Albany spot or any spot for that matter and Luciano could move in with supplying his dope from Italy to all the houses. And once its in the houses, it'll be no time before it makes its way to the streets."

"And what makes you think it'll be that easy." "Oh, no one said it'll be easy but everybody knows that's the way the world spins these days. You want something to sell or become popular then sell it through sex. But if Dewey catches his ass, he's already made it clear, that he's gonna' have Luciano's ass deported." Stanley could only nod in agreement.

"And that's where it's gonna' get really ugly. Cause neither one of them Jerks is

backing down..." "You betcha' fat ass neither one of them is backing down. And that's

why Luciano thinks he can use us to create his little disturbance, cause in the end he'll get

Dewey to back off to save his little upstanding image and whatever officers come in, shit,

they'll be on his payroll for sure. I'm telling you Tommie, I've seen this guy at work and

I'm willing to bet my life on it; that he's got one of his marksmen planted for sure."

Stanley thought long and strong about what his friend had said. And as much as he didn't

want to believe Dietz's jar brain theory it made perfect sense given the circumstances

they were under.

"We can't tell Luciano, no." He said.

"Not unless we got tickets to another country besides Italy." "Look, Dietz, give me a

minute. There may be a way to get the cake, the frosting and the ice cream. I'm gonna' go

down stairs and call a couple of people who could give us some manpower or some kinda

help in this thing. Help us out, you know....?"

Stanley immediately stormed out of the room and headed downstairs to the manager.

Upon approaching the front desk, an elderly man addressed him from afar. "Tommie.

Looks like someone's in a hurry." Stanley immediately plopped a twenty dollar bill on

the desk. "Need your office..." The elderly man smiled graciously after slowly sliding the

twenty dollar bill off of the counter and placing it in his vest pocket. "You know where it

174

is Tommie." Stanley made his way around the front desk and proceeded into the manager's office. He picked up the phone, wiped the mouth piece onto the stomach area of his clothing and proceeded to dial home. After several rings and no answer, Stanley had no choice but to hang up. Immediately he reached into his back pocket retrieving his bill fold. Stanley pulled out a small thinly folded piece of paper. On it was Phil Musica's office and home number in Stanley's normal chicken scratch writing. The numbers however, written on the paper were written in a coded system made up by Stanley. He always had a fear that if he were ever arrested, killed or caught in some kind of heist, the phone numbers would or could work against him. Therefore Stanley always wrote numbers down one less than the actual number. If the area code were 212 then he'd easily jot down 101 and if the prefix were 583 then scribbled on his paper would be the numbers 472. Stanley had made several attempts to get in touch with Phil with no success of ever making a real connection since the murders. Phil had called him back once or twice only to say that he hadn't forgotten him and that he was on his way into a meeting and he'd call him back. He would be in the city soon and they should hook up and have lunch and though none of those things ever manifested the one phone call within the long awaited time frame was enough for Stanley to believe in a man who had used him for his own significant and selfish reasons. His efforts in getting Phil proved effortless as well.

175

CHAPTER FOURTEEN

Several guests move quietly through the main lobby of the Claridge Hotel. It's Saturday approximately 03:00 PM and Al, the Hotel's manager has to deal with an irate prospect of a potential guest. A voice, stern but firm quietly blares from Al's office, "Hey! Ya' mind keeping it down a bit, please." Al hollers back to Stanley, "not a problem Tommie." The irate guest peeps over the manager's shoulder and in a very flagrant and arrogant manner asks, "And who might you be?" Stanley in his own rude but scuttle and direct tone simply replied, "Who me? I own the joint," Al, at this moment is doing everything to keep from laughing in the woman's face but is unsuccessfully able to do so. Not feeling the love or the grade "A" customer service normally given by the Claridge Hotel, the young lady storms through the main lobby and out of the Hotel. Al and Stanley both shared a laugh together.

"Tommie I swear, another stunt like that and you're gonna get me fired."

"Come on Al you do a great job around here. For years and nothing but five star treatment you give these people. You shouldn't have to put up with that shit from nobody. No matter how much money they got." Al acted as if he'd paused and actually gave what Stanley said some thought.

"You're probably right Tommie but in any event a little yelling from some snob chick ain't the end of the world for me. After all, if I ain't here that means you lose your office privileges." Stanley laughed but immediately apologized to Al from Al's desk. Although the rooms were perfectly equipped with guest phones, there were certain phone calls Stanley would not make from his room. In fact Dietz nor the hotel manager ever knew that where ever Thomas White was allegedly checked in at, Stanley Grauso was also checked in on the other side of town. It was his safe haven or ace in the hole you would say. Stanley always felt that if something went wrong with any of his Thomas White dealings or shenanigans Stanley Grauso could just change clothes and in the event someone would think that they saw him, his alibi of time frame and distance would always work in his favor.

"Your right Al, I guess that I thought this was my office or that I even owned the joint for a minute." "Not a problem Tommie. Hurry up and make your calls and get outta' here before my boss comes in this evening and sees you behind the scene, if you know what I mean. OH! And before I forget, pay your bill before you leave and I ain't talking about the hotel's bill for the room. Get my drift."

177

"Yeah I got your drift. If I ain't got anything else Al, I got your drift." Stanley's arrangement for running numbers and sharlocking from the hotel was quiet lucrative for Al. He always said that Stanley's contribution always helped him stay honest with his wife. "Ya' see Tommie, I give the old lady the pay check from the hotel and I keep the old pay check from you and Dietz for my own partying and gambling. What they don't know won't hurt em'? Right?" Stanley, often times listened to Al's gibberish without quite hearing him. As long as Stanley had what he wanted, friendships we're filled with smiles, laughter and of coarse, spreading the wealth. Sentiments, let alone, sentimental value rarely found its way into Stanley's heart let alone relationships.

After clowning a bit, Stanley found himself giving a call to home another shot. It had been weeks and still no answer. And while Stanley's absence and follow through with home seemed to have been procured by interests over the years, a part of him had began to worry. At some point he had began to think that the family was moving on without him intentionally, paying him back for his own intentional neglect over the years. In fact his last conversation with his mother had resulted in a not so good exchange of words due to Stanley's refusal of visiting his sick father. Mrs. Grauso in a painstaking manner asked Stanley to pull a five dollar bill and a ten dollar bill from his pocket and to look at them. When Stanley obliged her, she then asked in a sarcastic tone, "Call them mother and father and see if they answer back!" Then she politely hung up on him.

The phone rang.

"Grauso's residence..." said a distinguished voice.

"Who the hell is this," Stanley blurted. The voice on the other side ranted, "Who the hell s this?"

"Sal?!"

"This ain't no Sal! Who the hell is this! Who wants to know?"

"This is Stanley. Mr. Grauso's son..." Stanley seemed to have tempered himself a bit realizing that he had identified himself as Stanley with Al the hotel manager standing less than a few feet away. The gentleman on the other side of the phone paused for approximately a window of fifteen seconds after Stanley identified himself.

"Hello...hello..." Stanley had thought for a moment that he had lost a connection. The young man spoke. "Mr. Grauso's son....you Sure about that?"

"What do you mean am I sure about that? Who the fuck do you think you are!?" The young abruptly interrupted. "Cut the shit Stanley. It's me Freddy! I guess that would make me your younger brother wit' you being Mr. Grauso's son and all now wouldn't it!"

"Freddy?..."

"Don't Freddy me. You don't even recognize your own brother's voice. Has it been

179

that long Stanley or has it gotten that unimportant? Which one?" What could Stanley say

but..."Hey, how's everybody? Miss you guys." In a convicted but unconvincing way.

"Look Stanley, it is what it is," said Freddy. "I got no beef wit' you but you've hurt this

family so much wit' your selfish shit I might as well just come out and tell you."

"Tell me what?" Freddy covered the phone and looked over from the kitchen where

they had all once sat and ate as a family to make sure Mrs. Grauso wasn't anywhere in

sight. "Look, I gotta' keep it low so Ma' doesn't hear a freaking word I say. So listen

up!" The rhythm in Stanley's heartbeat seemed to have upset itself for a second almost

as if he were bracing himself for a bit of disturbing news.

"Salvatore is dead and on top of that dad ain't got long. Doc' says he can go any day

now as well." Stanley's heart dropped. An instant feeling of fatigue combined with the

slow death of breathless lungs came over him. Freddy's voice sounded as if it were in a

barrel with the BPM's cut in half on every word. Freddy had proceeded to tell Stanley

that Salvatore had been killed in the battle of bulge during the second world war at that

time. One of his rolls as a commanding lieutenant officer was to visually inspect and or

retrieve the carcases of fallen officers. And while going out into the field to visually see

for himself the body of not only a fellow officer but a friend as well, he too stepped on a

land mind and was killed. But with everything going on with Stanley and his father,

Freddy and the girls thought it best to only report that Salvatore was captured in an

enemy camp and that the United States Army assured that he was alive and were doing everything in their power to negotiate his safe return. Stanley, at first seemed to criticise

his brother and sisters approach in handling their mother's feelings and timid heart in the

matter of Salvatore's death.

"How dare you guys not tell her? I think, regardless of the pain, she needs to know."

"Who gives a shit what a part time son and part time orphan thinks!" Was Freddy's

rebuttal. Freddy made it clear to his elder brother that he wasn't in fact the little Freddy

Stanley used to smack around as a kid. In some ways as much as Stanley wanted to argue

and lash back out at his brother, he knew deep own that the family was right. In addition

to that, he just didn't have the energy to keep arguing after receiving the news about

Salvatore and Mr. Grauso. Freddy's Berlin Wall attitude was firm and fixed against his

brother Stanley. One could easily, including Stanley detect a smoldering volcanic

mountain of resentment in Freddy's voice and who could blame him. Stanley, after being

humbled had only enough energy to say one thing.

"Could you tell mom and dad I miss them Freddy?" After a small window of silence,

Freddy's tone changed but his mind frame and answers remained the same.

"You should really tell them both yourself Stanley. Tomorrow isn't promised to

anyone Stanley."

"Yeah sure..."

"So when..." Freddy asked.

"As soon as I'm done with things on this end Dietz..." Freddy realized that Stanley had addressed him as someone other than himself.

"What did you call me?" Without hesitation Stanley abruptly ended the conversation with Freddy, hanging up the phone. Ten minutes had seemed like hours passed and years lived coupled with precious time wasted seemed like only minutes when thinking about them. Stanley just stood in the hotel manager's office as if he were transported their by celestial means. As if he couldn't exactly remember his reality and how he'd gotten there in the first place. Voices muffle at a distance. The mentioning of his criminal surname brings him back to his reality but not enough to respond. His heart for a moment overflows with a bit of laughter thinking of Salvatore's famous words often directed toward him. "Mama's gonna whoop your ass when she finds out Stanley." His hand lands gently in the form of a balled up fist against the wall of the office.

"Always tried keeping me out of trouble...you'd think you'd be able to avoid a land mine Sal." Stanley's eyes well up with tears at a moment where his conscious is close to giving way to its edge. Slowly his body begins to fold giving way to its own weaknesses and vulnerabilities. The door curtain is briskly pulled back.

"There you are Tommie! Come on, who's got time to wait while you piss away time on the phone." A very demanding Dietz stood masking the office's makeshift doorway. It was as if Stanley's give way or clearance to reaching an emotional but cleansing side of himself easily became a plane for take off leaving without him as a passenger. Like a pigeon a stone's throw away from danger Stanley's concern for what morally mattered subsided. Dietz noticed Stanley's back turned toward him and the posture of his shoulders slouched in a most lazy and depressing fashion.

"Hey Tommie, you okay?" Stanley just abruptly stood up, turned with his head down and whisked passed the big guy.

"Let's go. Gotta get it Dietz. Don't worry about me, I'll be fine." He said clearing the emotional cob webs from his throat. Dietz, knowing his friend, could clearly see that something was wrong with the man he knew as Thomas White, however Dietz also knew two things. You ain't getting blood from a turnip and you ain't squeezing out of Tommie what Tommie don't whish to talk about. So in stride he simply shrugged his shoulders gesturing to the hotel manager that even he didn't know what to make of his friends sudden but brash behavior and followed behind Stanley.

The two barely spoke on their way to Troy New York. Dietz new that in a time where business had to be extreme to give his friend his space. The two had clearly taken over the five houses ordered by Mr. Luciano. Where violence was perceived as a tool needed, politics worked better. Dietz and Stanley had cut side deals with the madams and girls at the houses. In exchange for receiving the protection and the extended umbrella arm

183

of Mr. Luciano, he and Dietz had set up additional whiskey props within the houses. In that way, Mr. Luciano would receive his cut of what was made of the brothel end of the business while Stanley and Dietz side peddled booze and sharlocking deals preying on the vulnerability of a culture's immoral and driven sexual desire . He and Dietz both mutually agreed to pay back to the houses their share of what Mr. Luciano had guaranteed to them. In that way the houses weren't losing too much of a profit while Stanley and Dietz made out like a fat rat with their newly found side hustle. An all around win is what they called it. Clearly, if the information of their underhanded entrepreneurship made its way to Mr. Luciano's ears, a whole lot more than shit would hit the fan. More like shit and a whole lot of body parts.

Pulling up to the Troy house was a bit suspect due to a couple of cars following closely behind Dietz and Stanley. At first glance, it seemed as if the two cars tailing behind Dietz and Stanley a couple of Johns in need of services, however it became apparent that they weren't when two men stepped out onto the fixed porch of the house in a manner clearly stating that they weren't going to move from their position in blocking the door way. Both automobiles fixed themselves easily blocking the driveway in which Dietz and Stanley entered.

"Hold your horses.....don't jump to any conclusions and definitely don't get out of the car Tommie starting any shit." Dietz's eyes glanced over at his sidekick confirming his whishes. "You don't do anything unless I swing. Got it?" The dynamic duo had a system and code of ethics by which they moved in the case of a jam. Since Dietz was so big, his approach was always to show himself friendly and to immediately identify himself by lifting his hands in a surrendering fashion. He'd then always smile opening up his jacket showing that he was not armed. He and Stanley both figured that people would surrender their mistrust easily if the bigger man showed himself harmless. At which time if and when the opposing side became comfortable enough to let their guard down an armed Stanley would draw both his guns leaving Dietz to pounce during the element of surprise.

"Wait for me to swing on the two on the porch, then you keep the rear guys at bay when you draw both guns. If they so much as pick their noses Tommie blast their asses and don't stop till you run out of bullets or they're hit. Got me?" Before Stanley could answer Dietz exited the car and proceeded with his gentleman's act. At which time Stanley could see someone peeking from a window located upstairs. He was sure that he had seen the man's face the day when meeting Luciano. "This shit ain't right..." He thought. Stanley exited the vehicle and in a brisk but subtle manner patted his hips for good measure. Unfortunately this time he did not feel the bulge consistent with his guns being at his side. Immediately he remembered that he'd forgotten to return back to his room for his firearms and he and Dietz were now swimming up the creek without a paddle. There wasn't enough time to think, Dietz had already swung, knocking one of the men out cold. "Tommie show these bitches who the new boss's are," He screamed.

185

Stanley could only freeze while watching Dietz grab the second man who was clearly

awestruck by Dietz's line backing skills. Dietz must have clearly thrown the man fifteen

feet in the air away from the porch. It was useless screaming, "No body move!" While

reaching for guns that were not there but Stanley did it anyway hoping it would gain

some momentum for he and his partner in crime. Instead the two men taking up the rear

bum rushed Stanley knocking him to the ground hitting and kicking him profusely. As

Dietz turned looking at his disarmed friend, the man Stanley spotted staring out of the

window walked out onto the porch and quickly put one in the back of Dietz's brain.

Dietz dropped like a coat hitting the floor while missing a hook on a coat rack. The man

then stood over Dietz and put two more rounds into him. Stanley, in some ways, could

process what was going on in front of him but in some ways he couldn't. His body had

instantly become numb to the beating seeing his friend drop like a hot potato before his

eyes. At this moment it was fight or flight and the adrenaline rush within his conscious

could not and would not conceive the notion of death. The man who had maliciously

taken Dietz's life now had began taking steps closer toward Stanley. The sound of

muffled sirens could be heard blaring from a distance while growing closer. One of the

men quickly suggested to the man who had shotten Dietz, "Do this worthless sack of shit

and let's get out of here." The two men lifted Stanley to his feet while the hit man

hastened his steps and pointed the barrel of his revolver in Stanley's mouth and pulled

the trigger. The gun immediately jammed. With no hesitation Stanley thrust his knee headlong into the groin of the hit man. Leaping forward the two men were left holding

Stanley's coat while Stanley sprinted out of the driveway an onto the public road. The

men immediately jumped into their automobiles after him but Stanley had dashed through

an alley and cut off onto another side street where he had jumped into an officer's car and

made up a story that a gang of greaser kids had jumped him. The officer being a good

samaritan obliged Stanley and had taken him to the nearest hospital. On the way, the only

thing Stanley could think about was the image of Dietz's life size carcass laid out on the

ground and a statement that he was sure he'd heard one of the men make once he had

broken free. "Luciano's gonna be pissed!"....

CHAPTER FIFTEEN

For the first time in a long time, real tear drops graced the face of Stanley Grauso like a ballerina's footsteps gliding slowly across a well polished stage. His emotions were mixed and for the first time the foolish boy named Stanley Grauso and the even more foolish man surnamed Thomas White were in the same room meeting face to face and spirit to soul. The cops had taken Stanley's statements along with a fake name in regards to him being beaten up so badly and with Stanley's reports of a youth gang, greasers, they were called, being responsible all leads and points of any investigation were directed toward all of the local gangs. Stanley knew that few points of any criminal investigation were always revealed through the local papers and other pertinent points were somewhat exposed through word of mouth on the streets within certain circles. Anyone caught between the two could easily get a clear picture of what really took place and who it had taken place with. Stanley's hopes were to deter officers from knowing the real players involved in Dietz's murder. His statement and fake name given would also deter his colleagues in the underworld from knowing that he'd even whispered at a police officer let alone turned to one for refuge. He had returned to the Claridge Hotel and paid two months in advance, giving the hotel's manager the impression that he'd be staying a while. When asked about Dietz, Stanley mustered up enough phony to say, "Oh, he didn't tell you? I thought he told you that he was going out of town on business for a few weeks." The fact that there had been an unidentified man in the morgue fitting Dietz's description had to mean absolutely nothing to Stanley on the outside despite what it really meant to him and how much it was truly hurting him on the inside. Connecting himself in any way to his deceased friend, even if it were a call to a love one or a floral spread could mean him being contacted by police and or the men responsible for putting Dietz where he lay. Stanley just sat wondering aimlessly on the side of his bed. Next to his foot peeking its way out from under the bed was a draw string connected to a laundry bag. Stanley with his tears all dried out motioned his foot onto the drawstring and slid the bag from under the bed. The bag contained Stanley and Dietz's share of monies made between sharlocking and the cat house liquor profits, Thirty-eight thousand dollars to be exact. The two had a superstition belief that only keeping round numbers would keep the pot growing. They had done everything together, except died.

Stanley observed the money stacked and banded up in the bag. A part of him even wondered, was it wrong that his emotions would change from bitter to happy while observing the mountain of cash only weeks after learning of his brother's tragic death, his father's life threatening illness and after watching his best friend and partner in crime's brains completely blown out. Another part of him wondered while weighing his feelings in the balance for all three of his suffering loved ones was it wrong to long and hurt more for the one who in fact was not a blood relative. Wiping his eyes while slopping cold water over the traces of his dried tears from the hotel sink he thought about the conversation he and Dietz had the last time the two had counted out the money together.

"I'm gonna' take it all one day Tommie, I swear and put it on 'Damsel in distress'!" "Damsel in distress" was a horse who was always coming in second place by a nose in every race down at the BIG A race tracks in New York City. Dietz had lost only a fist full of money on several occasions on her but often times had stated "She always comes in second Tommie! One day no ones going to beat her. So it's up to me to keep betting on her. Save her so to speak." Stanley's thing wasn't betting on the tracks although he himself kept up heavily the action going on down there. Actually he had no choice. Dietz wouldn't let him forget it. "Why not?" He thought to himself, pondering the thought of granting his friend, who was now gone in the wind, one wish. Dietz had always said that he would go down to the track and wait right up until the very second before closing the window or opportunity to place a bet and put it all on his horse. That way any illegal hedging or fixing of the mutual would have already taken place.

"One fat bet at the last minute would offset everything," he'd always say. "And the one top cash in on that breaks the bank! And after that, they gotta pay Tommie! They

190

gotta pay!" His mind was made up. He was going to go all in. Split the bag and divvy up Dietz's nineteen thousand with all bets on "Damsel in Distress". But first, he had plans of going to the other cat houses where he and Dietz had set up for Luciano and cashing out one final time.

****

Between days passing and several stops made, Stanley was learning the hard way of what life was like without his personal body guard and friend Big Dietz. In addition he had been given the burden of carrying the woes of life without family as well, due to no one's fault but his own. It was right up until the point that he'd decided to place Dietz's share of their monies on a horse named "Damsel in Distress", that Stanley had made a conscious decision in calling home. Seeing and feeling the "life is too short" spiel baring down on his soul, it had become time, in his mind, to make amends with what was left of his family. As a result he'd found himself on a hiatus from the Big city standing alone with tears washing the headstone of his father's grave. Mr. Grauso had passed with none of his sons by his bed side or attending his funeral. With Salvatore killed in a war and Freddy recently arrested in a robbery attempt gone bad of heisting diamonds. Stanley's sister Dolly had informed him of the family's latest circus run. But unlike Freddy, Dolly didn't rain down fire and brimstone on Stanley for his neglectful and selfish actions toward the entire family. Her personality was more like their mothers; one sentence or phrase was enough to leave you to yourself as well as your choices in life. After which,

191

she simply gave Stanley the address to St. Michael's cemetery located in Stratford, Ct. And fished around with words as to some ideal time frame as to when he would visit their father's grave site.

"Why does the sun refuse to shine on the saddest of days?" He spoke openly at the grave. "Can you tell me that pops? Can you tell me that Charlie White?"

"Because there is no sunshine for those creating storms and havoc in the lives of others my son..." Stanley could hear the subtle voice of his mother walking toward him. He wanted to stand and immediately acknowledge her, however, being gripped by such degree of shame felt like a ton of bricks on his shoulders.

"Mom..." An aged Mrs. Grauso stood firm planting her heels behind her crouched son.

"Nothing has changed...I see."

"Come on mom, what makes you say that?" "You still can't face me. When you were a kid I always knew when you were up to no good because you'd always make it your business to avoid me. This time there's no room to run to and no father to cover you Stanley."

"Who told you I'd be here?" At first there was a small window of silence but Stanley interrupted before Mrs. Grauso could speak.

"Never mind. Tell Rose she's getting a fat lip for old time sake." Although Stanley chose to contribute laughter to his own joke, it was evident from the silence and the sudden chill in the air that nothing was worthy of any laughter from Mrs. Grauso.

"You come to a grave for consolation? Why Stanley? There is no life here. There is not even your father here. Just the remains of a tent that housed who your father was. And nothing in you says that there is life at a place you once called home." Stanley huddled over with more contentment and shame pulled his hat from his head balling it up like a piece of paper pulled from the typewriter of a writer overwhelmed with writer's block.

"Stand up and face me, Stanley. Turn around and face me like the man you should've become long ago." Angered by a mother's true words, Stanley did just that. His frustrations were obvious and the eye contact made by he and Mrs. Grauso spoke volumes. A son seeing the years gone by through the crows feet planted in the corners of his mother's eyes versus a mother's wrenching heart seeing how life has changed and beaten her son.

"You look like grandma..." Stanley said speaking softly.

"And you...my son look a mess." Both had made a little wiggle room for a smile. Stanley began to feel as though he were worthy enough to speak to his mother. Gathering his thoughts, he spoke.

193

"You know Ma' I am a man...you know?" Mrs. Grauso wasn't sure if Stanley believed his own statement.

"Come home son. Please...." Stanley looked as if he were giving his mother's proposition some thought. "Please..." She reiterated. "Before there is more blood on your hands or before your very own blood is in the streets." Her words haunted Stanley. Wether it was the tone in his mother's voice ringing with what seemed to be a prophetic resonance or talking about blood and death over his father's grave, Stanley countenance seemed to change dramatically. Looking over to his right at a distance was his father's old automobile with Dolly on the driver's side. She had driven Mrs. Grauso to the grave in hopes of making a final plea with her son and brother. "Look at me Stanley...is that too much for a mother to ask. Stop looking over at Dolly. Dolly's shaded image and blank stare through the car's window seemed to pierce Stanley's very soul. It was as if he were being confronted by his mother on the left and on the right.

"What choice do I have? There. I'm facing you. You're happy now?" An elderly but strong Mrs. Grauso and a confused and torn Stanley seemed to play tug of war with their eyes. Each one with their own will toward the other. "I have no time to play games Stanley. I have no sons left. Do you know what it is like for a mother to live sonless?" Before Stanley could speak Mrs. Grauso interrupted him. "Maybe this is my punishment and curse. Who knows?" You can come home now and at least I can have a son around the house."

194

"You mean a man around the house?" Stanley jokingly reiterated.

"When I walk away you walk away with me now, today or go back to this Thomas thing you have." Stanley's eyes widened a bit. "Yes I know more than you think I do, Stanley. So what's it gonna be?"

"I'll come home..." Stanley replied with a serious amount of hesitancy. "...But first, I gotta take care of something...or some-things you can say." Mrs. Grauso shook her head. "It's still got a hold of you. So maybe it's where you belong. And maybe I have to live with that."

"No I promise! As soon as I...."

"Stanley, you and I both know that the one or two things that you HAVE to take care of will turn into many things and many days and I'll never see you again."

"Mom I swear..." As Stanley spoke Mrs. Grauso turned slowly and began to walk toward her car.

"You can follow me if you like Stanley...." She whispered. However, the distance between the two grew further and further with Mrs. Grauso entering the automobile on the passenger's side, Dolly pulling of and Stanley being left at the grave.

****

Going back to New York wasn't easy for Stanley. In fact, if it hadn't been for the train ride back home he wouldn't have had reasonable time to sit and think about where he was in life, in addition to where he was actually headed. For once, his conscious had bothered him and his mother's voice rang true in his head and had some significant meaning bearing down on his soul. "Before there is more blood on your hands or your very own blood in the streets," rang over and over in Mrs. Grauso's voice. In addition to, "I'll never see you again..." A part of him felt like he owed it to his mother in granting her wishes due to the fact that he'd been so negligent as a son to her and Mr. Grauso but more along the fact that he'd fail in something as simple as making it his business in coming to see his father during his last days on earth. And while those feelings were sometimes good to fathom as well as feel, they weren't enough to bring about commitment or better yet, a change of heart. It hadn't been a full week and Stanley had already embarked on an agenda that clearly stated he wasn't headed back home, let alone giving one ounce of thought to Connecticut. With more trouble ahead, one would think that Connecticut would be an easy choice but for Stanley it was as simply put as Mrs. Grauso's statement, "It clearly had an unresisting hold on him".

Stanley immediately after settling foot on New York soil headed back to the Albany cat house. It was there that he had ran into a prostitute nicknamed "paint". All of the guys and girls even called her that because everything from a dress to a bathrobe fitted her soothingly as if it were painted on. Her real name was Chloe. A rebellious girl from a good

196

home and middle class upbringing gripped by pure stubbornness, mixed with two parts of laziness and "know it all", was her components and make-up. Her side of the story concerning her life always played her as the victim but one could easily see when dealing with Chloe, that she easily made victims rather than friends. What she wanted was what she wanted in addition to all that mattered in her own twisted little mind and no cost was to high to pay. Stanley's timing however, couldn't have been more perfect in returning to Albany. In his mind he was going to see Dewey and Corky in hopes of getting a sit down with Mr. Luciano on explaining what happened with Dietz being murdered and where could he possibly go within the organization from there. He was coming up through the driveway that he and Dietz had often sat out in discussing their next move within Luciano's circles or sharing a laugh or two. When suddenly belting out of the cathouse and into the driveway like a bat out of hell was Chloe. Stanley had grabbed her dipping off into the street and into an alley.

"Keep quiet toots!" He said holding his hand over her mouth. Chloe was too overwhelmed in a panic of hysteria kicking and screaming.

"Look toots! You better keep it down or whatever done run your ass out of that house is gonna find you. Now keep it down." Chloe calmed down a bit upon recognizing Stanley's voice.

"Tommie, what are doing here?"

"What do you mean what am I doing hear. Checking in! Gotta get things back in order." Chloe just starred at Stanley as if he were a non English speaking American abroad and totally lost. He continued, "So what's got you running? Some drunk john giving you a hard time?"

"Never mind me! You better get your ass outta' here now Tommie!"

"What do you mean get outta' here? Nothing's doing! Is Dewey in there. I gotta go and let them know Dietz is dead. We gotta regroup....As Soon as I kick this john's ass for you." Chloe grabbed Stanley as he motioned in the direction toward the house.

"Are you stupid or the last to know. All the girls here know Dietz is dead. We were just wondering were you dead with him!"

"DEAD WITH HIM?! What the hell do you mean dead with him?"

"Tommie, I swear you didn't hear this from me..." Stanley let Chloe go. As she turned he could easily see that she had been badly beaten. Her lip was extremely swollen and her ears dripped with blood from her ear rings being pulled out. The straps on her dress had been torn leaving her own arms and hands as its support system. Stanley stroked his hand gently across her bruised cheek taking notice of the blood vessels badly burst in her right eye.

"What do you mean am I dead Chloe and who did this to you?"

198

"We gotta go! I will tell you on the way but I'm getting out of here on the next train smoking!" The two soon hopped in a cab headed for the train station. Chloe remained quiet during the ride there gripping Stanley's hand the whole way. Her eyes clearly were readable, insinuating to Stanley or Tommie as she had known him not to utter a single word. The two exited the automobile and Stanley paid tipping handsomely.

"I think we should go into the city instead of taking the local."

"This will be fine. I'm going back home. This is it for me." Stanley observingly stressed with his eyes pointing toward Chloe's entire attire.

"Look, let me take you and get you cleaned up. You can hide at my room and at least I can give you some money to help you with your trip and all. You just gotta be straight with me Chloe. What the heck is going on! And who did this to you."

"Corky did.....she found out that I was doing Dewey."

"Doing Dewey? Are you crazy..." "That ain't the half of it Tommie. Dewey and Luciano are behind the shooting that got Dietz wacked. They were really looking to off you totally!" Stanley's jaw dropped. His thoughts and words both played catch up before forming complete phrases. Like that of a stuttering baby.

"Ho' shit! They found out about the extra booze me and Dietz were skimming. I never thought they'd want to kill us for pennies? Break our arm maybe?"

199

"What are you talking about? Booze!" Stanley attempted to explain the run that he and Dietz both were enjoying with setting up shop within the cat houses he and Dietz had confiscated for Luciano. Chloe immediately interrupted. "No one gives a shit about your side show hustle Tommie. Corky and Dewey both are responsible for everything that's gone bad." She explained to Stanley that the shit he was in was above head far more than knee deep. Chloe dropped a bomb on Stanley. Dewey in times past recently had explained top her that Stanley and Dietz's troubles were due to Corky's need of blame to be shifted from herself to someone or others less relevant than her. Dewey wasn't one to hold back from running his mouth after sex. People in politics often joked that if Dewey were a prisoner of war he'd be tough enough to survive. However, if they ever put a girl on him no secret in the government would be safe. Stanley's heart fell listening to Chloe explain that Corky had informed Dewey that Luciano had been importing heroin and dope into the cathouses and the results were utterly chaotic with violence escalating, the girlz along with their johns getting hooked and everything becoming run down. At the time Dewey was gearing up to run for attorney general and needed no stress connected with the escalation of crime. According to him that would only give his opponent a shoe in for another term. He and Luciano had already began bumping heads banging the same woman, Corky, and all and neither seemed to respect the other or bring it up. As a result Dewey finagled it some how and scheduled for Luciano to be arrested and scheduled for deportation for up to one year. When Luciano found out Dewey, in order to protect himself and Corky, concocted a story along with Corky, blaming Stanley and Dietz for exposing Mr. Luciano's heroin movement. Dewey explained to Luciano that a tip came from the Albany house into the New York police precinct and that an ongoing secret investigation had been conducted and that there was nothing he could do. It was out of his hands, when in fact, Dewey and Corky were the real source of the tip and had said that undoubtably they knew that it was Tommie and Dietz. The result was Dietz life with Stanley escaping by a thread.

CHAPTER SIXTEEN

Only a few days had passed since Stanley's conversation with Chloe. The two had spent the day together up until the evening and bid each other fair well. Stanley had thanked her for the inside tip on Dewey and madam Corky's bull shit that had lead to the slaughter of his best friend. Stanley had given her the money to get back home to her parents and made her promise that she wouldn't make the mistake of looking back for fear that somewhere along the line she'd be deterred giving in to the lifestyle that she had known to be right when it came to provision and welfare for herself.

"No way fore a young lady to live..." He told her, as the two departed. But who was he to tell Chloe what was best concerning her relationship with her parents when in fact he himself had traded what was left between the bond of a mother and son to be where he was then. Stanley deep down could see himself in Chloe but after listening to her account of her life story and the change of events that landed her beaten and bruised in need of enough money to make it home he drew this conclusion.

"I can't believe you had an old man that actually did everything for you to succeed." Chloe in her stubbornness Stanley's judgement, "Who are you to judge me or tell me that I'm wrong about my father?" "All I hear kid is your dad wanted you to get good grades and make something of yourself and that was too much for ya'. My dad....said the same thing to me. The only problem was that his actions and what he let me do spoke a lot louder than his words. Trying to put things together or at some point of perspective in Stanley's head didn't for once seem hard. Stanley pulled what was known as the "Oki doke" on Chloe. he had given her close to a thousand dollars for her trip back home. Stanley pulled out an even fatter knot of money than the one he had given her earlier.

"Gimme' the money I gave you earlier." His body language insinuated that somehow he was going to give her the much larger amount loosely clinched in his right hand. Chloe with her eyes bulging from her head instantly conceded handing over the money in her possession. Stanley instantly snatched the money from her and shoved both wads into his pockets. When asked what was he doing he simply told her, "A kid like you don't need any extra money cause somehow I feel like you won't exactly make it home if you ain't hit rock bottom." With that said Stanley put her on the next thing smoking with only enough money for a meal and the next transfer of fare. He would never know where she'd end up but for once and for her own good, even a "blind" man like Stanley could see that it was his responsibility to make every effort in getting this shell of a woman back into the care of her parents without the smallest remote chance of setting up shop elsewhere.

****

It wasn't long before Stanley had cleared all of his things out of the Claridge hotel and made his way over to the Big A race track. It was his way of honoring his fallen friend, clearing his head and hanging his life in the balance based on whatever happened that day. Standing at the ticket window with all of Dietz's share of the money, Stanley slid the suitcase into the compartment that wasn't barred and to a man he referred to as Molly, he stated "All of it on 'Damsel in Distress', and hurry the race is about to start." Molly opened the suitcase and surprisingly enough gesturing his eyes back and forth between Stanley and the money. A smirk was all he sported because truth be told, people came in with that type of money quite often.

"You ain't never came in with this type of dough before kid. Wait a second..." Molly went into the back, picked up the phone and uttered to the person speaking on the other end, "Yeah, get Abbadabba up here....fifteen stacks on the next fly." It wasn't long before a middle aged man good looking in stature made his way from the back office to the ticket window. Molly motioned the middle aged man over to Stanley's suitcase for a thorough review of the funds. Periodically the man would look over at Stanley while fenagling the money in the case with his left hand and his right hand flatly placed on the outside of his right pocket. Rumor had it that's where Otto Berman kept his steal always

204

standing at an angle where he could watch you out of the corner of his eye while handling whatever business.

"Nothing personal kid, just business..." he said looking over at Stanley. Otto looked over at Molly and spoke softly, "Tell Lansky, to make sure the race is held and take the bet."

"You got it, Abbadabba," said Molly. Otto walked over to the window.

"Where's the big guy you're usually with when you come." Stanley stumbled his words. He definitely didn't see that question coming nor could he assume where it was coming from.

"Come on kid! The real strong looking heavyset guy I usually see you down here with. You two are like peas in a pod. Where is he?" Stanley, still stumbling over his words, immediately went with his gut on not telling this man anything.

"Oh! He's outta' town on some other business for a little while. I'll be joining him soon."

"Leaving town after the race?"

"Yeah. Something like that." After learning what he had learned about Luciano, Stanley realized he didn't know who Luciano knew. All he knew was that he had gotten word that somehow, Dewey and Corky had convinced Luciano that Dietz and Stanley had something to do with Luciano's pending deportation and arrest in connection with alleged and attempted dope trafficking. And the fear of it all weighed more heavily on him due to the fact that this world was the only thing he'd ever respected in his life and to know that he'd possibly and soon enough could be a prospect of the hunted frightened him beyond measure. Stanley soon made his way out to view the race after receiving his ticket from Abbadabba..

"And when you don't win, you could always use the back of this ticket for writing out ya' grocery list!" He said while laughing at Stanley upon handing him the receipt. Stanley walked away looking back periodically. Otto Berman just smiled repeating what he'd always say to any client losing money big or small.

"Nothing personal kid. Just business." In fact that's all it was. It was his business. Otto Berman was a known mathematical genius who knew how to win at whatever expense when it came to fixing the numbers as well as the outcome of any race. His sharp whip was a combination of tactful and evil when it came to money. A native of New York, Otto, "Abbadabba" Berman, like Stanley was always in trouble. Even at the young juvenile age of fifteen, Otto Berman, was arrested and tried for attempted rape but somehow managed to beat it. Sources close to Otto growing up often said that it was beating that rape case that gave Otto the haughty disdainfully personality trait of always believing he could "cheat the future". His relationships were a majority of people who smiled in his face and cursed him behind his back. It had been quoted out of many mouths as to saying, "One day life's gonna catch up with old Otto and say to him what he's been

saying to everyone else. Never personal, just business!" Hate him or love him, he

definitely was the apple of his boss, Dutch Schultz's eye. The money that Abbadabba's

con game antics brought in was lucrative, quiet and definitely under the radar. In addition

to being a wiz at fixing races and numbers, Otto was also a damn good accountant and

keeping his reputed mobster's boss's money out of everyone's business, including the

IRS, surely caused Dutch Schultz to use added muscle and influence in keeping any

alleged enemies off of Abbadabba.

Walking out into the bleachers seemed like a taskmaster's task to Stanley. The weight

of his emotions had really started to take its toll on him mentally and personally. The

horses had started out of the gate and it wasn't clear where Damsel in Distress was at the

time due to the emotional haze he'd been experiencing. It wasn't long before a man much

taller in stature than Stanley appeared beside him. Stanley didn't say much as the man

leaned over the rail while watching the race. Stanley did however think to himself, "This

guy's a little to close for comfort." But instead of causing a ruckus, Stanley just simply

slid over and began rooting his horse on who appeared to be gaining a lot of steam while

coming around the stretch. "Come on baby...." He motioned quietly clinching his fist with

all intensity and greed. Stanley suddenly felt the discomfort of the man next to him

stepping on his foot. This time it was apparent that the man had intentionally invaded

Stanley's space.

"What the fuck is your problem sir? You drunk or something?" In a matter of seconds, the man turned quietly and discretely with all of the racket and ruckus going on and opened the right side of his jacket revealing a pistol neatly tucked in his pants.

"My problem....is that I missed when I killed you're friend and I'm usually a better shot than that....." Stanley's nerves were shaken.

"Don't even think about budging or running. Mr. Luciano, wants to have words with you." As Stanley stood frozen with fear the man pulled a small piece of card board from his pocket.

"I was told to give you something..." With a dead smirk on his face the man pulled from his pocket what appeared to be a ripped up train ticket. Before handing it to Stanley, he wiped the ticket gently across Stanley's face, crumbled it and shoved it into Stanley's right hand.

"What's this?" Stanley asked as he wiped a wet smear from the side of his face the man patted the ticket on. In as much as he could Stanley attempted to look into his hand without taking his eyes off of the man, not knowing his next move. The wet smeary substance appeared to be small traces of blood.

"Let's just put it this way! Chloe won't be needing it anymore..." A cold chill came over Stanley.

"Chloe's dead?!" Stanley stood looking at the man as if he were for some odd reason expecting an answer. The horn continued to blare with the announcer's voice calling the race still in progress, "And it's Damsel in Distress coming around the stretch, now by a nose....."

"Look...." Stanley said to the man, "I ain't leaving with you just like that. I ain't gonna' just lay down and draw a freaking bulls eye on my belly or my head and say shoot me...."

"You'll do what the f....."

"Or what?" Stanley bolstered. This place is too packed for the both of us to start shooting this bitch up and make it out alive or not being caught by the cops..." The man's sudden body language seemed suspect of Stanley's idle threat but it was the only weapon he was holding at the time. Stanley thought it best to reassure the man, "That's right, you ain't the only one holding..."

"Look I told ya' Mr. Luciano just wants to talk to you..." The announcer's voice blared continuously, "It's Damsel in distress in the lead.....Now it's Damsel in distress by a neck. Trouble T falls behind coming to the finish line....And The Damsel claims one finally for herself. She won't be in distress much longer...Damsel in distress has done it. What an upset for Trouble T."

At that moment Stanley knew he heard what he'd heard but couldn't let on dealing with a loaded pistol pointed dead at him while bluffing that he too was armed.

"If I see you so much as flinch or look like you're gonna reach for your steel, fuck the cops and everybody around me, I'll blast you to pieces." Stanley thought quick and fast. "Look, I'm sure Mr. Luciano is paying you rather handsomely to bring my head back in a bag but how bout I double what he's giving you to walk away. You know give me time to hike outta' town."

"That might work fat boy except for one thing..."

"Oh yeah, and what's that?"

"Mr. Luciano already told me not to come back if I don't get you and he ain't kidding. If I don't do you, he's gonna have me done and everybody knows you ain't hiding from that killing squad he hires outta Chicago." Stanley sweat profusely.

"Look ....."

Before he could get another word out edgewise, a firm hand rested on the back of his right shoulder squeezing it firmly. "Hey kid, you're horse came in on that ten to one, like a freak accident. We gotta' talk. Dutch is going to be pissed but hey, that's my problem...." Stanley turned, the voice speaking was that of Otto Berman himself. Otto suddenly noticed the man standing in front of Stanley. Surprisingly enough he knew the man.

"Phil what are doing here. Luciano got you scoring things out trying to get in on the action..." he said jokingly. "Look tell your boss Dutch will kick his ass for meddling..." The man Phil smiled keeping his eye on Stanley. Stanley did however, take notice on how uncomfortable Phil had become when Otto showed up. Stanley turned fully facing Otto and spoke secretly through his teeth, "Tell your boss, he can keep the winnings just get me out of here..." Abbadabba spoke firmly, "Is everything alright here Phil?" Phil nervously gestured with an unconvincing laugh, "Why wouldn't it be? Abbadabba!" Stanley twitched his head in the smallest of fragments gesturing No, that things weren't in fact all right. "Well look here, the kid here's coming with me. We got some business to sort. See?" Abbadabba, stated. Phil attempted to speak in a manner of squaring off against, Abbadabba's wish but soon found his words cut short. "Listen, cut the shit Phil!" Abbadabba interrupted pulling his blazer to the side revealing a handgun tucked away in the waste of his trousers . "The kid and the Dutch got big money business with this guy here. So tell your boss unless he want problems with the Dutch, to back off." Phil hesitantly flexed, "Look Otto, you know Luciano ain't gonna back down from nobody, not even the Dutch. Especially over no rat. Now the kid's a rat and rats have to be dealt with! Now I want no problem with you and you think this kid's worth Luciano and Dutch getting into it over?" "At a ten to one odds with a hundred and fifty thousand big ones being the pot? Yeah, I'd say my boss would want that kind of problem any day.

Phil's expression clearly suggested that he didn't have the foggiest idea of what Abbadabba was talking about concerning money or as put, "A hundred and fifty thousand big ones".

"Look, Abbadabba...." Before Phil could get another word in edgewise, a short stout man, well dressed with dark hair could be seen walking toward the suppressed commotion. Abbadabba spoke, "Look here Phil, here comes Dutch. My advice, would be for you to look over your shoulder and in front of you at a distance." Phil gazed off into the directions given by Abbadabba. "All of those guys you see are packing some serious steel and they all got their eyes on Dutch making his way over here. I wouldn't advise you to so much as flinch." A small trickle of sweat seemed to make its way out of Phil's facial pore. The short stout man made his way over to the gentlemen. "Hey, Otto, conducting a meeting and didn't invite me?"

"Hey Boss...." Abbadabba addressed the man as "boss". In fact even Phil's body language seemed to address the Dutch, as he was known with the utmost respect.

"Hey Boss, you remember Phil don't ya." The Dutch glanced the man over at first view.

"You're one of Luciano's boys right?" Phil nodded. Dutch then sternly retorted, "So what the fuck are you doing in my establishment. Charlie knows what I said about spies." Abbadabba then leaned over and whispered something into the Dutch's ears. Stanley

212

couldn't make out what exactly he said in its entirety but he could hear the phrases, "ten to one and keep the kid alive." Dutch then looked at Stanley. "Sharpie, you having problems with this guy...." Stanley didn't know what to make of Dutch's words but simply went along with it. "Yeah Boss..." Dutch referred to Stanley instantly as "Sharpie", because he was taken at how sharp Stanley was dressed. "So look, Phil unless you want to go back to Luciano with no fucking arms I suggest you beat it!" Phil's expression suggested that it wouldn't be that easy but what was he to do being out numbered. Bowing out gracefully in order to live another day to fight again, Phil left quietly. The Dutch and Otto Burman both grabbed Stanley and whisked him away into Dutch's office and commanded that extra security be placed at the outside of the door. Otto Berman let out a loud burst of cheer screaming to the top of his lungs. Once in he headed straight for the bar in Dutch's office and began pouring his boss and Stanley a drink. "Drink up kid. Here's to saving your ass!" Dutch took a huge swig of the potion Abbadabba had stirred and gasped.

"Now would somebody tell me who the fuck is this kid and why we're saving his ass by putting our necks on the line for him...."

"Come on Boss! You know you loved sticking it to Luciano's boy. Tell me you would've done it for a buck!" Dutch then blurted, "I would've done it for a quarter!" The men both then blared out laughing and soon the other men in Dutch's entourage, who were allowed behind closed doors joined in. Dutch's demeanor was crisp. Stanley

213

definitely knew from talks within circles who he was. But even though he had gotten out of Luciano's grip for a moment he wasn't really sure pairing up with Abbadabba and the Dutch was exactly the right move either. For all he knew, the men could do away with him just the same and never pay him, let alone take the money as a payment for protection. It was like having money in a bank during the time of the Great Depression stock market crash. Sure its yours and the account for all intense and purposes has your name on it but good luck in getting it! Dutch Schultz, formerly Arthur Flegenheimer, was known as a criminal and nothing but and at the time had to have probably been the most well known criminal of his time. His ruthlessness and violent temper spawned him up the criminal ladder making him Public Enemy #1 by the FBI. Born in 1902, Schultz began with common petty thefts and assaults, and by the age of 17, he had graduated to more serious crimes, including robbery. By 1919 He was convicted and sent to a juvenile penitentiary where he served 15 months. Afterwards, despite numerous indictments and arrests, he never again served time behind bars afterwards. Following his release, he quickly resumed his former occupation and criminal past times. This is when he first began using the name "Dutch Schultz", that he lifted and appropriated from a legendary deceased New York gang member. By 1925, Schultz had become both criminally successful, and politically connected. Using money and violence, Schultz quickly gained control over unions and the "Numbers Racket", or what was known as the "Policy Racket", an early and illegal version of the lottery. His criminal empire had spread rapidly

214

into Harlem and parts of Manhattan where he too, like Stanley, discovered "Bootlegging".

He also discovered like Stanley the rivalry that came along with the territory. Vincent

(Mad Dog) Coll, would prove to be just that. He was a former associate who matched

Schultz in both temperament, talent and criminal wit. Their fight, bloody and long, lasted

for years and had claimed many lives until Schultz ordered him gunned down by three of

his men while in a phone booth in front of a Manhattan drug store. Unlike many within

the rackets, Schultz's hand of power didn't halt with the end of Prohibition in 1933. His

control increased his influence at Tammany Hall which at the time was known to be the

seat of power for the at the time corrupt Democratic machine which controlled the courts,

the police and just about everything else in New York City. His name had easily become

a common everyday phrase in the mouth of FBI director J. Edgar Hoover. With New

York's finest refusing to pursue him due to inside corruption, the only charges that had

come down at the time, but did not in any way slow down business, were charges of tax

evasion which led to a trial. Dutch's lawyers, who included a former U.S. Prosecutor and

a former New Jersey Governor, successfully argued that he could not receive a fair trail in

New York City. The approach to his defense was simple but effective. The government

had just brought down another notorious gangster by the name of Al Capone , making the

same charges of tax evasion stick. And with a feud brewing on the cusp between he and

Luciano things were bound to take its toll for the worse within the circles of the mounting

criminal cesspool.

215

The men shared a few drinks and Dutch finally popped the big question. "So tell me Abbadabba , why's this thumbtack worth saving let alone in my freaking office?" Stanley's facial expression clearly expressed his lack of like in being called a thumbtack. "Don't worry about it kid, its a compliment." Abbadabba stated to Stanley. "He calls people who dresses better than him a thumbtack. You know, 'sharp as a tack!'"

"Yeah it's a compliment kid. Not that I give a shit wether you like it or not but it's a compliment." a very tipsy Dutch Schultz reassured Stanley.

Abbadabba then explained to Dutch the huge fortune owed to Stanley because of the small plethora of cash plopped down by his new found friend. In between Abbadabba explaining the situation of the ten to one pie out of the sky, Dutch didn't hesitate in making his feelings known concerning Luciano, Dewey and Corky. The conversation spawned all feelings of hate and revenge in sync and with Stanley able to give Dutch and some of his boys secrets pertaining to all three, Dutch's organizations help and protection would come easy for him. Stanley also explained the assassination attempt made on his life and how he himself wanted nothing of his One hundred and Fifty thousand dollar winnings in return for a shoe into Dutch's world and a chance to kill Luciano, Dewey and Corky in return. Dutch walked over to Stanley and invited him into a secluded room apart from his office. One of his men patted Stanley down and escorted him for a private sit down with Mr. Arthur Flegenheimer himself. When the door shut Schultz's smile went cold while Stanley's smile hung out there like a wet shirt waiting to dry.

"So tell me kid. Why shouldn't I believe you ain't one of Luciano's spies sent over here to break my bank. Give me one good reason why I shouldn't have you dropped out of a window on your head and just keep the money anyway?" Stanley's thoughts froze. "And if your reason ain't a good one....I Hope you brought yourself a helmet." "Cause I can take the money I just made you and take it down to the IRS in DC for your tax bill. It'll make the charges and the future trial go away..." Dutch Schultz immediately grabbed Stanley slamming him against a wall.

"You trying to play me for some kind of joke kid!"

"Not at all Mr. Schultz. Everybody knows and reads what's going on in them papers you see. And at the same time, everybody loves you here in NY see....so, With it being a legitimate win it won't hurt you if some people in the good old city here got together and pitched in for a fund or some type of aid because we love ya and with it being a gift it can't be that bad, if bad at all on taxes...."

"You can do that..." "Yeah, my dad used to do it all the time. Pay taxes from a sudden gift. They'll give you a lot of shit at first but, after a while they'll take it and if they don't it'll definitely hold things up until some type of plea deal is offered." Dutch let Stanley's shirt go.

"You better not be shitting me Sharpie!" Stanley could tell that there was more of a soft side for him with the Dutch because of the gestures of nick names still being thrown around.

"Call your attorney and ask him. Now I don't profess to be some expert but this is a legitimate gift if the person who won it is still alive to explain in fact yes he did give it to Mr. Schultz the philanthropist." Both men laughed. Schultz called one of his men in to get in contact with his attorney. After speaking to him Schultz was advised that in fact it was worth a shot due to the low risk of explaining or tracing that kind of money's inception. "I guess you'll live kid...at least for now anyway."

CHAPTER SEVENTEEN

It wasn't long before Stanley and his new boss hit it off. Between running numbers and handling bets Stanley had already proven himself in becoming a little cash cow for the Dutch. Sealing the deal in proving his loyalty came when Stanley himself volunteered to take the one-hundred thousand dollars in cash to the IRS building in Washington, D.C. Eventually he was turned down and sent back to New York by way of train carrying the bag full of money. The mere fact he returned back with all one-hundred thousand dollars in tack and not one dollar missing showed the Dutch he was as honest as they came in the criminal world.

"All people do is steal from me..." He once told Stanley. "The thing that pisses me off isn't that they steal believe it or not. Shit, we're all criminals, but that they act as if I don't know....like I'm freaking stupid and that's where the trouble comes in for their asses at." Stanley would periodically joke with him saying, "Boss I'm going to always be a gentleman by letting you know ahead of time when I'm gonna steal from you." In return

the Dutch would always reply with his sarcastic gangster rhetorical gestures saying

something in the neighborhood of, "And Sharpie, I'll make sure I'm a gentleman in the

same way by always letting you know wether I'm going to put a bullet or a foot up your

ass, you know?" Stanley's sense of Humor sometimes was a defusing mechanism for the

Dutch's temper at times toward the other guys. Sitting in meetings with the Dutch's mos

t important men made Stanley feel like a big shot. It was sporadic but rarely did he

venture out into the streets with Berman or Marty Krompier, one of the Dutch's

lieutenant. Otto and the Dutch kept him close like a baby, never too much activity out

and about due to the on going beef surging between the Dutch, Luciano and Dewey. Like

an open three-way love triangle gone sour between agreeing partners, Dewey seemed to

operate and move like a jealous lover thrown out of a circle cheated by lust. Some of the

troubles brewing and rumors stirred within both circles seemed to actually come from

either Dutch's or Luciano's end when in fact they were sewn or planted by Dewey's

paid spies within both circles. Dewey had already set things in order for Luciano's

deportation back to Italy and the fact that Stanley was still alive flaunting his stuff

around like an untouched hooker within Dutch's circle seemed to grow like an ingrown

hair bump under Dewey's skin. Either way and whoever would strike first, a mess in

New York was brewing and bound to hit therefore affecting every crime ring within the

big city of lights. Rumor had it that a part of the Dutch's protection over Stanley had a lot to do with his hatred toward Dewey's mistress Corky. No one ever heard him say it

but anyone in fact everyone would speculate or assume that the Dutch had feelings for

her himself. The word whenever he wasn't around was "There must be gold in them there

hills to have three criminals ready to kill." Them hills of coarse being made in reference to

Corky's underwear. And with no way of resolving his ongoing tax evasion case or even

getting the courts to bend a little, unlike Luciano, Dutch Schultz was unwilling to sit idly

by while Thomas Dewey placed chains on him using his political influences from within.

Dewey knew that if he'd stirred up enough trouble that it would be a matter of time

before either side would fire first. And if that strategy didn't work in those days ongoing

beefs affected the totem pole within the criminal world therefore affecting the next

criminals income. The result would be what was known as a virtual bounty which was an

untraceable pool of money offered on ones head. The way the underworld saw it was that

if the FBI and IRS was on one then it would be a matter of time before the FBI and IRS

fever would spread. A virtual bounty was the easiest way to turn friends into enemies

and with as many enemies as the Dutch and Luciano had it was only a matter of time

before colleagues and other criminals wanted both out of the way to lay seize to New

York's criminal throne.

****

The stress of it all was really starting to get to the Dutch and everyone around him

was starting to feel the brunt of it all. Everyday it seemed that his criminal empire grew in stature and so did his personal fear, worry and mistrust for the people around him who had not only helped him get to where he was but in addition had guarded him from those against him.

"I got to get out, get some air! Who do these sons of bitches called the law think they are." He said to Stanley. "Let's get out for a minute. Forget everything for a second, the case, the IRS, money, everything." Stanley asked, "Say the word, where to boss..." "Thirty fourth, for a simple cup of coffee....some laughs and some peace."

"I don't know about that boss. New York has been pretty hot these days. You got crazies out there who don't know the difference between you and that clown Luciano these days. He ain't never to far from there and I think it can get a little crazy." Marty Krompier agreed with Stanley, "He's right boss. Word has it that there's already been several shots taken at Luciano's boys since he's been back from Italy."

"When did that ass hole get back..." Berman shouted. Stanley interrupted suggesting of a place often visited in Newark New Jersey.

"Look why don't we get away right over the bridge. There's a cool little spot called the Chop House. Drinks are delicious and they even put a little whisky in your coffee for some kick. Food ain't bad either." The Dutch panted for a while as if he were persuaded in taking Stanley up on his suggestion until the loud moths of the bunch, Landau and Rosenkrantz spoke up,"Ain't no one telling us where and where not to go. This is our city boss. And if you want a cup of coffee on thirty fourth then whoever tries to stop us.....we'll wipe the whole street with their ass!" Dutch and his ego agreed and since he was the boss then it was what he said that was final.

The guys sat around for the most part shooting the normal gyp lingo. In fact, the owner of the place had given the spot strictly to Dutch and his boys for the rest of the afternoon. He left the key with Marty for him to lock up. Before leaving however, the phone rang and while no one could discern the words spoken on the other end or who they were spoken by, a look of serious concern and a serious change of demeanor came over the owner. Immediately after hanging up the phone the owner shouted, "Hey Dutch, we gotta get outta here. That was one of the boys from the fifty-eighth precinct ....HE SAID.......TO TELL YOU......." Before the owner could finish his sentence shots rang out from the outside of the shop. Glass breaking and bullets flying everywhere. Because the blinds had been closed due to the owner closing down early, no one could see the likes of who was this borage of bullets was coming from. Marty and the boys began firing back. The Dutch drug Stanley to the floor and Stanley grabbed Otto on the way down. "Stay down boss!" Otto shouted. Dutch along with Stanley crawled over and hid behind the take out counter where Stanley suddenly noticed he'd been hit in the shoulder. The man shake profusely at the sight of his own blood.

"Calm down, we'll get you some help when the smoke clears." Stanley said assuring to the owner. The Dutch handed Stanley his hat urging Stanley to use it as a compress over the owners shoulder wound. Stanley put the hat to the shoulder of the wounded man then shouted, "Marty, Lansky.........YOU GUYS OKAY?!"

"YOU STAY YOUR ASSES DOWN AND WATCH THE DUTCH!" Marty screamed. It wasn't long before the sound of bullet riddled glass and chaos soon dimmed itself in the ears of Stanley. Seeing the blood of the owner smeared over his own hand he soon thought to himself, "What did this guy do to get shot? Except extend his place to the boss. It wasn't long before the vision of his conversation with him standing at the grave with his mother seemed like an oil painting in the smeared bloody wound of the young man with his mother's words or warnings ringing loud in his psyche.

"In the kitchen area....." Panting like a deer in need of a flowing river brook, the owner spoke to Stanley. "In the kitchen....in the back..." Stanley immediately urged the owner to take it easy and not to speak. "Don't press yourself. We'll get you and the Dutch outta' here shortly. "Sharpie, I think he's trying to tell you something....." said the Dutch. The gun fire had simmered down an become less sporadic by now. Shots rang out every now and again. Stanley tuned in the owner was trying to say to him.

"We can get out through the kitchen. It leads to the cellar and we can go out through the back entrance." Stanley immediately cried out to Marty and Lansky, "Boys hold your fire we got another way out. Let's go before the cops start moving in." Marty and Lansky immediately dashed over toward the counter where Stanley and the Dutch along with the wounded proprietor and lifted the almost fallen soldier making their way to the back with Stanley covering the Dutch. The wound the owner suffered wasn't life threatening although severe hitting him badly in the shoulder. Stanley took him to a hospital over the bridge somewhere in or around Newark, New Jersey. After the man's family was notified, Stanley ditched the hospital in an attempt to avoid having to answer to any police authorities. It wasn't long until he met up with the Dutch and the boys. When Stanley walked in he witnessed for the first time Marty and the Dutch in a somewhat heated discussion.

"All I'm saying boss is that there's no way to prove absolutely that it was Dewey. I don't think that was a good idea...you always told us yourself, don't fuck with the courts and cops....!" The Dutch recanted in screams. "THIS SHIT HAS DEWEY WRITTEN ALL OVER IT! HE KEEPS FUCKING WITH ME AND NOW I'M GONNA' OBLIGE HIS ASS!" "What's going on?", Asked Stanley.

"The Dutch, just ordered a hit out on Dewey. He even asked Luciano to help stating that it would be best for both organizations." Lansky reported. "You think I'm crazy too?" He asked Stanley. "Or you scared for your ass like these two pussies?" Stanley was at a loss for words. Deep down he knew that the man he'd grown close to was wrong and that killing a man or even attempting to harm a man like Thomas Dewey would bring the entire U.S. Federal government authority and agency down on every man and even a tic if he were involved.

"This guys trying to get the death penalty or something! Straight suicide!" He thought to himself. "I SWEAR ON MY OWN SOUL! HIS LIFE OR MINE ONE OF US WILL BE DEAD IN TWO WEEKS TOPS!"

"SO WHAT IS IT SHARPIE! YOU IN OR NOT? ANY BODY NOT WITH ME LEAVE NOW, IF YOU CAN LIMP YOUR ASSES OUTTA' HERE FULL OF HOLES!!!" Stanley thought for a second but deep down knew to say yes would be planning his own funeral and while he himself had done it all it was at this very moment when life simply meant something to him.

"Of coarse I'm in boss. ....But..."

"BUT WHAT....."

"You say we have two weeks right? We gotta' think this thing this thing through....." The phone rang. Otto picked up.

"Boss it's for you....."

"WHO IS IT!?" "They say its Chicago calling and please calm down Dutch before you blow a fuse." Dutch rushed to the phone. "Finally some real help!" He murmured motioning to Otto that he would take the call in the back away from Stanley and the boys. Otto followed.

While the Dutch was in the back handling the mysterious phone call from Chicago,

Stanley, Lansky and Marty engaged in small talk as if the walls had ears. Each man wanted the others take on their out of control friend and boss but skated on thin ice in terms of any phrase or word being taken as disloyalty. Each man spoke in a low dialect under Dutch's shouting which could be heard from the other room.

It wasn't long before Schultz came storming out of the back with Otto not far behind with his hands extended as if he were pleading with the fleeting wind.

"I'LL KILL THE BASTARD MYSELF!" Dutch shouted repeatedly. As Stanley, Lansky and Marty approached the fire breathing dragon, no man's tone or voice of reasoning could be heard.

"CAN YOU BELIEVE THIS SHIT! ALL THE BUSINESS I GIVE THE BOYS OUT IN CHICAGO, THEY WON'T TOUCH THIS BUM WITH A TEN FOOT POLE FOR ME! I TOLD THEM ALL TO GO AND SCREW THEMSELVES FOR ALL I CARE!" With himself caught up in an uproar like a fly wrapped in a spider's web the Dutch motioned grabbing his chest as if he were in an insurmountable amount of pain.

"Boss you okay?" Otto quickly stated.

"Sharpie get the Dutch some whiskey. Hurry!" Marty ordered. Stanley did as he were told making the Dutch a glass of Scotch.

"You okay boss? Come on let this shit go. Look at what it's doing to you...." As the

Dutch slowly took the glass of Scotch from Stanley he sat down slowly in a two seater living chair assuring the boys that he was okay. With a few deep breaths and a couple of sips of his top shelf Scotch, he continued. "I'm not letting this go. The fact that no one is willing to come to my aid tells me it's going down any way!"

"What's going down Boss?" Marty asked.

"They're going to kill us all..." Dutch's reply sent a cold through the room like an overworked air condition unit.

"But it ain't gonna be without a fight...." The Dutch then looked to Stanley staying silent for a minute.

"Sharpie, you go back to Connecticut for a while. This ain't really your fight."

"What do you mean it ain't my fight boss. You guys are like family to me. You saved my life and that makes it my fight..."

"Yeah, let him stay or come along! Sharpie's a pretty good shot..." Marty replied. Stanley agreed. "Listen to me...." The Dutch interrupted. "I know this shit like the back of my hand. We let Sharpie go and spy out new territory cause after we take care of these bums we're gonna all have to leave the big city and set up shop elsewhere. And why not Connecticut. We can take over out there and still keep an eye on what's going on here." "Pretty smart Boss!"

"Yeah that's why I'm the Boss!" For once the fellas shared a laugh. "Sharpie you go and visit your mother for a while. Tell her your thinking about coming back home and settling down and in a few weeks I'll come out there, case the joint with you and we'll set up shop." Stanley agreed.

It wasn't long before Stanley found himself on the train back to Connecticut. Truth be told he was glad in a way to be heading back to Connecticut. His fear and loyalty of being portrayed as a rat easily made him say yes and commit to the Dutch in helping him get rid of Dewey but deep down Stanley knew a person had a better chance at drinking rat poison and surviving than becoming poster boys for a governments' war on crime. He had spoken with his mother and told her that he'd wanted out of his life style and that he just wanted to practice being the son he'd never been with whatever days he had left on earth. Mrs. Grauso had agreed and was overjoyed but had told Stanley that if it was true reconciliation that he wanted then no fragments or pieces of his life could be brought within arms reach of the simple life she had now become accustomed to.

"That was the one mistake I made with your father Stanley. Thinking somehow that evil and greed sewn outside of one's home could never make it inside of one's home. Not so!" Her words spoken were firm and had no room for reasoning. She continued, "Your father and I definitely reaped what we've sewn. He often said that his suffering was just and in every groan and agony of pain said he had it coming and often begged the Lord for forgiveness." She went on to tell Stanley that she had promised Mr. Grauso that if she took another husband it wouldn't be someone in the criminal world and not to let his

daughters do what his sons were allowed except Salvatore. So when Stanley had made it

back to Connecticut all of his things, friends and history associated with his life and

lifestyle, he took with him to the Stratfield Hotel located in Bridgeport CT without Mrs.

Grauso's knowledge. Pretending to come home empty handed and being one that had

given it all away for the sake of sanity Stanley stayed a few days a week at his mothers

carefully selecting his wardrobe and vernacular when in her presence. She believed his

alibi of working at a hotel in Bridgeport as a bellhop and dishwasher in order to make

money. Truth was in fact Stanley ran a small numbers racket soliciting local government

employees. With Mrs. Grauso not being able to get around much his alibi would prove to

be a shoe in with his mother and his sisters who rarely bothered with Stanley at all

concerning his life over the years and weren't going to start any prying now.

****

Weeks had run by adding up to months. Stanley's communication with the Dutch and

the boys had become far and few in between. By now he had left over fifty messages

with Otto for the Dutch to give him a call. Otto explained to Stanley that Schultz had

been laying low and rarely in New York and that they were often meeting at the Tavern

spot he'd suggested in Jersey. New York had become foreign territory after a large beef

had surfaced with gangsters in Harlem. Dead bodies were turning up and despite evidence

or word of mouth surfacing amongst the streets the Dutch was being blamed. Otto had promised that he would get Stanley and the Dutch together soon. Stanley had found some

cops in the Bridgeport area willing to be on the take staking out potential locations for

setting up shop. But even Stanley at times when talking with Otto wondered if Otto

knew the real whereabouts of the Dutch or had spoken to him. His stories seemed to

change whenever Stanley questioned him in a tell all run down fashion of what was going

on.

It was a Sunday afternoon and Stanley had come from dinner with his mother and

sisters. While standing at the courtesy desk of the Stratfield Hotel he asked, "Any

messages..." The man standing behind the desk shook his head slightly responding, "Nah

no messages but you did have a visitor." Stanley wondered who could've come by to visit

seeing that he had just left his mother and sisters for dinner and when it came to the

Stratfield location none of his sharlocking clients and number racket people knew of it.

Off hand the description given to Stanley by the hotel clerk didn't register and Stanley

had began racking his brain as to whom it could've been. Suddenly but subtle a firm grip

pinched Stanley between the neck and right shoulder. A cold chill surged through his back

down to his ankles. He recognized the chemistry or surge of energy felt from the grip. As

Stanley turned he heard the voice of the clerk grow faint, "There he is sir, that's the

gentleman who came for you earlier." For a moment Stanley stood frozen not knowing

wether to embrace the man standing in front of him or not. It was the Dutch. He

whispered, "Not here..." Removing his hat he continued, "Where can we go and talk?"

231

Stanley then escorted the Dutch up to his room where the two could talk. From the moment they entered the room, Stanley went on and on about locations and future dealings for taking over the city. "Sharpie, stop. Stop it now. There ain't gonna be no take over. At least no time soon anyway."

"What do you mean, no take over. If there's no take over then what you come here for boss." Said Stanley.

"I gotta hide for a few days but I need you to do something for me. Not Lansky, Otto, none of them."

"Sure boss anything, what do need....? You name it!"

"I need you personally to kill Dewey. I thought it all out. No one knows you where he lives. He takes his kid to school every Thursday morning see. So the morning he's having breakfast getting ready to take his kid, he grabs the paper off of his step. You can whack him then! We set it up to where you change clothes and change cars and your out of there." Stanley plopped down on the bed at a loss of words.

"I'm sure the cops that they have on occasional stakes in the neighborhood knows all of our guys but they've never seen you..." Stanley thought for a moment about the conversation he'd had with Otto earlier. Otto's statements and time lines concerning what he'd revealed to Stanley about Dutch didn't coincide with the time frame of the Dutch

232

being able to make it into Connecticut.

"I haven't spoken to any of the guys in a while. What's going on with everyone." Said Stanley to the Dutch.

"We've been meeting at that Tavern spot you suggested over in Jersey. Only meet twice actually but the beer and food is great. Last couple of weeks everyone's been laying low at my word." The Dutch leaned in closer to Stanley. "I really think they got the boys from Chicago in on the hunt for us."

"What do you mean by they? "I think....NO! As a matter of fact I KNOW, Sharpie. That Luciano and Dewey and the boys out of Chicago are all working together to get at me."

"Who are these boys in Chicago?"

"They're known as Murder Incorporated.....contracted killers. And none of them think that this schmuck deserves a pine box." Everything the Dutch was saying seemed to be a little too much for the Dutch to take in. His paranoid demeanor had never been seen by Stanley and although Stanley knew nothing about the contracted killers in Chicago it was enough for Stanley to back off seeing how they had the Dutch shaken up and paranoid. Regardless of his tough talk undeniably so, he was standing in front of Stanley looking for a place to hide and there was no stand up tall talking about being ready to die. There was simply a man who's birth name was Arthur Flegenheimer endowed with the spirit of Dutch Schultz a notorious gangster that had been stripped from him. No longer feared like a deme god of this world and now vulnerable like humanity oppressed and ruled by its inadequacy to rule forever Dutch and Arthur both stood in front of Stanley suspended from the vessel that both had occupied and contended for residency in for years. His vulnerability and humanity seemed to even rub off on Stanley.

"Dutch lets get a good night sleep and figure this all about in the morning."

"Your not willing to help me are you?"

"Its not that at all boss. But we can't go to a gun fight with our fists..." Stanley rose from the bed and made the Dutch a drink from a makeshift stash or bar spread from his dresser. The two drank and the conversations seem to take a less tenacious turn. Soon the evening had passed and so it was for the week and by then Stanley had been introducing the Dutch to a few of his colleagues as if he were some celebrity. It wasn't long before wind of the Dutch's presence had made it to Mayor McLevy, a reputable politician at the time who thought it necessary to even pay Mr. Schultz a visit. McLevy was known not to be in on the take so to speak but only warned the Dutch that there had better not be any trouble.

"The city's been through enough corruption and violence and as you can see this is the result. We need to think about what's best for the city. Now while your here, I can't tell you that you can't be here but if there's one ounce of trouble, then I'll make sure your stay is cut short." Soon after McLevy's visit, Schultz had become paranoid and thought it best to take off. Stanley tried convincing him not to go back to New York but was unsuccessful in doing so.

"Are you coming or not?"

"I can't say that I am Dutch....." Stanley spoke sadly. "It's one thing to fight and become a casualty in a war but its a whole different level running in the middle of a battle field with no armor. These guys aren't playing Dutch and good bad or indifferent Lansky and Otto are right. We don't need to start an all out war behind foolish hate. Let's come out here and start over. Build our army and live to fight another day. Dutch disagreed but still agreed that Stanley keep with the city for a few weeks and he'd soon return. The two parted and Stanley wished his friend the best. Two weeks had gone by and while Stanley wasn't a big TV person he kept with his normal tradition of coffee and the Wall Street Journal. That morning while picking up his coffee Stanley went for the usual taste first sip and a quick glance scald himself by dropping his coffee clean in his lap viewing the Headlines. SCHULTZ IS SHOT, ONE AIDE KILLED. At first glance Stanley perceived that the Dutch was only shot but reading on learned that he too along with Otto, Lansky and Marty were all murdered. The news hit Stanley like a ton of bricks but his emotions remained stable knowing deep down the news did not unexpectedly seem unreal to him.

While his heart hurt his well of tears seemed to have run dry seeing that for once he had made the right decision in not going with the Dutch back to New York. A part of him felt bad seeing that the men were all gunned down at the Tavern Newark cafe Stanley suggested but even his conscious dismissed the aspect, "They would've found those guys anywhere..." he thought to himself. A part of Stanley thought more about the buried money and treasures often spoke concerning the Dutch. His mind raced as to where or how he could get to the items or even find them but rested with the truth of that if Dewey or Luciano ever saw his face again they'd remove every hair from his head manually before killing him.

"Kill or be killed...!" That's what the Dutch always said but for once its real meaning rang in Stanley's mind and that's "Kill and eventually you'll be killed as well!" It is with those final thoughts and the death of a fallen criminal hero Stanley Grauso knew life On The Lam no more.